# Life More Abundant

Part Three of

## A Trilogy

Part One – I Came
Part Two – That Ye Might Have
Part Three – Life More Abundant

## Other Writings by Walter Lanyon

Available through:
Mystics of the World
Eliot, Maine
www.mysticsoftheworld.com

# Life More Abundant

Part Three of

## A Trilogy

## Walter Lanyon

# Life More Abundant

Mystics of the World First Edition 2015
Published by Mystics of the World
ISBN-13: 978-0692352533
ISBN-10: 0692352538

For information contact:
Mystics of the World
Eliot, Maine
www.mysticsoftheworld.com

Cover graphics by Margra Muirhead
Printed by CreateSpace
Available from Mystics of the World and Amazon.com

ೀ ಌ

Walter C. Lanyon, 1887 – 1967
Originally published 1940

# Contents

A handful of dust could hide your signal when I did not know its meaning. Now I am wiser; I read it in all that hid it before. It is painted in petals of flowers; waves flash it from their foam; hills hold it high on their summits. I had my face turned from you, therefore I read the books awry, and knew not their meaning.

Where roads are made I lose my way. In the wide water, in the blue sky there is no line of a track. The pathway is hidden by the birds' wings, by the star-flies, by the flowers of the wayfaring seasons. And I ask my heart if its blood carries the wisdom of the unseen way.

— Rabindranath Tagore

# Chapter I

# Conquest of Fear

Fear can manifest itself only because of a belief in separation. As long as you are something apart from God, you will experience, in one form or another, fear. It is subtle and hidden, like a poisonous serpent coiled in the grass, liable to strike at any time—at the most unguarded moment, when least expected.

Its only power is given to it by thought, and it can be swollen by thought from a serpent into a dragon. All thoughts of evil are like toy balloons in that they are enlarged until finally the capacity is overtaxed and they burst. Sooner or later a fear will explode itself, however much or little damage it has done.

*The panacea for all fear is your union with God.* This is not a mystical thing, as believed in former times. We are now in the New Day, where the things of Spirit are realities and the things of matter immaterial and transient. The moment you are separated from Me and wander into the thought-world (the vacuum of separation), you are subject to the laws of fear—fear of life, of disease, of debt, of people—and all these fears are backed up by plenty of evidence and tangible proof.

The one who is filled with fear sees the "ten thousand fall at your right hand" and is so convinced of the reality and power of evil that he fails to notice the one who passes through unscathed. Like a bird charmed by a serpent, he is so magnetized by the evil that he cannot escape, yet if he were to break the spell (thought) for a moment, he would find that he had within himself a way of escape—he could fly, he had wings. But the little bird (or you) sits and looks at the terrible specter, thus giving it power—in fact all the power it has. It (and you) become so terrified at what you see that, unable to use your only means of escape, you are destroyed.

> The moment the thought about a fear is broken, the means of escape is apparent.

Taking flight sounds like a simple little means of escape from something so terrible, but it stands. Jesus knew how to do this very thing. He immediately "went unto the Father" and became *one* with Him, and then the belief in a separate power disintegrated, and the manifestation of evil vanished.

The enemy comes at you in one way—and is delighted to get away from you in ten ways, if it can. It has been so sure of itself because of your acceptance of it; but when the brightness of this union of you with God takes place, the blinding, disintegrating light causes evil to flee.

"Stand and see the salvation of the Lord" has a definite, positive value to you *now*. For you are beginning to sense-see the power of being *One* instead of two. You are beginning to appropriate the instantaneous relief felt from this *Oneness*.

This sudden appropriation of *Oneness* is accompanied by the consciousness of how to eliminate the object of, or the belief in, fear. There are different "cities" of refuge into which you may run for every differing degree of fear; yet all are the same God. This running" into God is not as symbolical as it appears. It is an actual fusing of you with the Father within you, and from that moment, you are a majority, and you will know the nothingness of the fear belief.

It is wonderful—yes, awesome what can take place the moment this union is made. The former things and their powers are as nothing; all are dissipated and destroyed. Whatever manifestation persists in standing in the way of your on-going must and will be destroyed. It makes no difference how much the human mind is inconvenienced; Oneness will permit nothing that "maketh a lie" to remain.

So "put up your sword." The currents of Life, the *one* Life, are flowing through you and finding expression through the newly extended senses, and that is sufficient to illuminate any darkened condition.

The Philistines (state of consciousness) built up a great ogre—even as you and I have done—and finally gave him so much power that the entire city was to be destroyed; but there was a way of escape. David and his five pebbles brought the ogre down.

You, with your five senses extended into their spiritual capacity, are more than a perfect match for any giant of fear that can confront you. At the glory of His coming, all the earth trembled.

The glory of the Lord is being revealed.

The thing that you fear is sure to come upon you, one way or another. It may never have an embodiment in the flesh—it may be a rankling, devastating, unseen fear which never comes to actual manifestation—but it is just as powerful and has come upon you just as definitely as if it had a body and menaced your on-going. The thing that you fear, you hate, and the thing that you hate, you fear; and so the cleansing of the mind from hate takes away much of the value of fear.

As you intensify your fear by terrified thought and continued contemplation, it grows larger and more all-conquering until you "remember your Father" and run into *Him* quickly—and then you see the sudden deflation of the balloon of appearance. It is as if the great swollen thing were run through with a rapier. It has not time to escape; it is destroyed.

No more are you trying to match God's power against the power of human thought. You come *with* the Power, and every other pseudo-power is over-thrown—devitalized and made nothing. If it will not let go easily, it is taken out of the way, together with its manifestation. It makes no difference into what confusion the false belief is thrown or to what chaotic state of mind it is reduced—the thing that it has tried to bring into manifestation now becomes its own undoing, and your enemy is left to handle and come out of his own beliefs.

The blessing of the Lord takes from him once and for all time any power over you and is the cleansing agency that enters into the cesspool of his mind and starts a cleaning that is not perhaps as happy as it might be. You see again that you are not matching God against the tough and violent power of man. It is as nothing. He blows His breath upon the appearance, and it is consumed as a feather in a blast furnace. It is nothing.

Fear is engendered in the human situation by the recognition of a power opposed to God, which is able to bring down on you things that you cannot avoid, perhaps that nothing can avoid. When you view the power of God, it is ruthless and terrible and awful to contemplate, in one sense of the word. So "the fear of the Lord is the beginning of wisdom," for it is the beginning of the end of human fear. And it is instantly productive of the fruits of peace and quiet.

The nervous, excited mind that is beside itself, like a storm-tossed ship at sea, suddenly experiences "a great calm" as the Master speaks to it, "Peace, be still." This is Power; and the illustration of the fear at sea (the man in his own consciousness, being tossed about like a frail craft in a storm) is perfect. The illustration is given to show you how instantly all the human laws are reversed or made naught. With the power to speak, "Peace, be still," comes the instant manifestation. Do you recall how Jesus did this and how He said, "The works that I do, ye shall do also, and even greater"? Do you dare to "come to me" on the waters of disbelief? Can you accept this glorious gift of God?

"Fear thou not, for I am with thee: be not dismayed; for I am thy God: I will strengthen thee; I will help thee; I will uphold thee with the right hand of my righteousness."

Is it any wonder that the "sons of God shout for joy"? Is it any wonder that within you goes up such a paean of praise and thanksgiving that you suddenly precipitate a rain of blessings, so many that you cannot receive them? Is it any wonder that you are glorifying and magnifying "the Lord in the midst of thee?" No. You can no longer keep from this joy of the Presence, the moment you turn unto Me.

Turn unto Me!

Call upon Me!

Come unto Me!

Every one of these is an invitation to escape instantly the dire evil of human fear. You can and will learn to run into your city of refuge, and the fury of the human thought will spend itself like a flock of evil night-birds that dash themselves against the Light that is shining in darkness. Suddenly you are that Light; and the evil manifestation, which had been urged forward by the impetus of its hate and your human-thought support, destroys itself and falls into the ocean of oblivion.

This is the truth—it could happen literally if it were necessary. Or the thing could cast itself into the swine form and rush on to its own destruction. You see, we are entering into the New Day—the day of revelation and manifestation, the day when we can say naturally, "I believe," because, having experienced the instantaneous transmutation of things when we "run unto Me," we become the majority which this Oneness gives.

"It is I; be not afraid." Do you hear? You have nothing to lose and everything to gain, for the most you could lose would be some negligible matter formations; and what they represent can be brought out again and again, and more perfectly, if the consciousness of them remains with you.

"It is I; be not afraid." You begin to see this *I* standing in the midst of the evil situation, and this very recognition disintegrates the thought-form, or mask, that has been hiding it from your view.

We arrive, finally, at the point which is so full of the acceptance of God that it can and does say, "Even if You slay me, yet I will say You are God" —and the last stand is taken. Even if You slay me, yet will I acknowledge this One and Only Power.

It is wonderful to know that we are beginning to sense the Power of it (the instantaneous ability to accept and make manifest the words of Jesus). At first this may seem a little confused, and you will go back to the things you have given up. But you will find nothing there. You have "come out from among them." You are free and shall walk fearlessly into the New Day, pushing out the "borders of your tent" farther and farther—daring to take more and more of the Consciousness and accepting It as natural and real and true.

"Praise the Lord, O my soul, and forget not all his benefits." All the benefits of this Lord, this Father, this Oneness—they are as the sands of the sea; to try to count them is hopeless, impossible.

God is even in the midst of hell, for "if you make your bed in hell, there am I." If *I* am not recognized as there, you will burn to death—but if you recognize Me, *I* will manifest to you heaven. Sounds foolish?— but there it is, and it can be and has been proven. So this recognition of the Presence here, there, and everywhere causes one to see the sudden change that comes when he is able to "look again, and see the fields white with harvest."

God in the midst of the dead Lazarus was what enabled Jesus to bring him forth. The Father, the Permanent Identity of Lazarus, was able to pick up his body from death and putrefaction and bring it forth perfect, for he had life everlasting, and Spirit was present in every cell and fiber of his consciousness. This had to be recognized before it could take place. The sudden union of Lazarus with God—Life Eternal—was made, and the army of beliefs, however time-honored, put to flight.

Do you begin to understand what it means to see God in evil, in hell, in the devil, in sickness, and in fear? It gives you the power of Oneness, for if there is any place God is not, then your God is not omnipresent; there is a vacuum, and another power must fill it. These vacuums are like pockets of evil which must be cleansed by the daring recognition that God is in the devil. "The wrath of man shall bless thee." Do you hear? Your very enemy is to bless you. Why? Because you have called out the God in that bewildered maze of human beliefs, and He has come forth.

"You do not need to fight." "Put up your sword!" "Set yourself and see the salvation of the Lord." Can you do it? You can, when the Love of God has entered into your heart and your recognition of Him as here, there, everywhere has been made.

Separated from God, you are naked and afraid, and you try to hide from Me (but can find no place where *I* am not). If you go to "the uttermost part of the earth, there my right hand shall lead you." If you "take the wings of the morning," if you do anything the human mind suggests, you cannot escape Me. And this recognition of Me as *here* and now present is enough to untie the knottiest human law that was ever conceived.

All this, "by a way ye know not of" and can never find out, for in every instance, it comes by way of a different manifestation. You will cease to speculate or wonder how it can take place—that is no concern of yours. Suffice it to say, it will take place in one of those natural ways that are so mystifying to the human thought that it flees in abject terror from "the brightness of his coming."

When you are one with Him, you are a majority, and you are one with the brightness of His coming.

"Who did hinder you that you should not obey the truth?" At long last, you will answer, "I hindered myself," because I believed I was something separate from God, that I had a life which was disconnected but which could be momentarily joined with Him through affirmations or prayers.

It is like magic—the quick and sudden change of everything—when the Lord is recognized as being in the terrifying situation that confronts you. If this be an incurable disease, He is there, awaiting recognition. True, He may apparently be covered over with an avalanche of human beliefs. But all this covering is nothing but so much mist to the brightness of His coming. And at this coming, the mist is absorbed like water poured on a burning desert.

"I am with you" all ways as well as always. *You have this instant panacea with you.* It is there, awaiting recognition. Nothing is too small, nothing too great to put through the fire of His brightness. Nothing can stand in the way of His coming, and His coming takes place whenever you can recognize this Presence as everywhere, instead of in an imaginary heaven.

Finally you will understand the Love divine that is a part of you—the Love of this God who is everything to you and who is instantly available and ready to neutralize all your ills. The deep love and sacred acceptance of this wonderful Power finally becomes an actuality.

You will not love Him emotionally but with a deep spiritual fervor that lifts you above mortal fear. This is the perfect Love that "casteth out fear" and is recognized *now* as impersonal and automatic. It is this love that you can bring to another in the throes of some terrible panic or fear. This love covers him like the soft feathers of protecting wings. Within the folds of this Love there is no fear; and there is no hate or misunderstanding. For the brightness of His coming into being has destroyed all untoward conditions, together with their manifestations.

"The fear of the Lord is the beginning of wisdom." "Perfect love casteth out fear." *What have you to fear after you know Me?*

> *I* am with you *now*. *I* am with you always— and the laws of sin, sickness, and death, fear and evil are no longer potent. They have collapsed and are no more. "Fear ye not, for I am with you."

# Chapter II

# The Higher Order of Beings

> If one advances confidently in the direction of his dreams, and endeavors to live the life which he has imagined, he will meet with a success unexpected in common hours. He will put some things behind, will pass an invisible boundary; new, universal, and more liberal laws will begin to establish themselves around and within him; or the old laws be expanded and interpreted in his favor in a more liberal sense, and he will live with the license of a higher order of beings.
>
> — Thoreau

Integrity is the keynote to the higher order of beings. Without a sense of this, nothing worthwhile can take place.

A recapitulation is necessary to find out just where you stand. Do you seek Me for the loaves and fishes, or for the miracle (the Power)? Are you still believing that you can get something out of Me? Or will you come and "take all"? One will be the distorted human life, the other an entering into your divine heritage, where you are not surprised or excited over that which you know to be true, simple, and natural.

"Behold, the old order passeth," and you are facing this very decision. To enter into the order of the new being, the old order of the John Smith consciousness must pass away. You do not hesitate to let go of something which has brought nothing but confusion and futility into your life—or do you? Is there anything you wish to salvage out of the wreck of personality with which you have been struggling all this while? Is there name, family, position, importance, race, creed, or anything that you are trying to save? It is all as nothing and will pass anyway—so why waste time trying to perpetuate these worthless things?

"You are a new creature in Christ Jesus." In the New Day into which we are entering, you are a new creature, and if you hope to "do the works that I do," you will have to recognize that a "new creature" is not burdened with old, outmoded beliefs, however Nothing will finally "save your darling from the flames." For it is this very darling (personality) which has caused you so much difficulty, and now it is to be consumed in the fire of Spirit, and with it are to go all the rags of self-pity and self-importance and all the rest that it has hugged to its bosom. You are a new creature in Christ Jesus. Over and over this repetition is made in order that you may understand "what the Scriptures say unto the churches (temple-bodies)."

You are entering into the place of Power, wherein the Word accomplishes without fail and is not something which is fraught with mere hopes and wishes. This *Word* can only proceed "out of the mouth of God," and the Christ Jesus Consciousness is that mouthpiece of God through which He manifests Himself and speaks and brings to pass everything that is to be accomplished in the New Order of things, which is even now enfolding you.

"If one advances confidently in the direction of his dreams... ." This lovely bit from Thoreau, fraught with such light, indicates what begins to take place when this new consciousness of "flesh" has come to you. There is a marked change in the wavering, vacillating human thought, for suddenly, the consciousness of the flesh moves or "advances confidently" into the place of its "dreams," of its desires.

"Advances confidently" — do you understand what this means? The old human consciousness can do nothing confidently, for the moment he, with Wolsey, thinks, "Good, easy man, full surely his greatness is upon him ... there comes a frost, a killing frost, which nips his roots, and he dies as I do,"

There is no security in the human consciousness. You dare not make a single statement. You cannot say you will be well and happy this time next year and that you will have plenty, because you know that even while you are speaking the whole picture may be changed and you may be reduced to the very opposite of this desired state. So the poor, fearful human thing knocks on wood, or it prefaces everything it says with, "I don't want to brag." Imagine bragging about the gifts of Spirit, which cannot be changed by a thousand years of thinking or meandering about in the human mind.

"Come boldly to the throne of grace" is not within the capacity of human thinking. It can come boldly to nothing but its little victory of the moment, and even then it has to be guarded by an almost invincible bulwark of human power.

"The old order passeth away" as soon as you recognize Jesus Christ, and the "former things are forgotten," and finally they are so dissolved into nothingness that they disappear entirely, even from memory. The old order is passing right now with such rapid strides that you can begin to say to yourself something definite and tangible. You begin to cast your burden on Me and bring away a blessing. It is wonderful. You begin to advance "confidently in the direction of your dreams," for a new strength is with you, and as long as you keep your attention on the Power, you can and will walk on the waves, literally or figuratively, and arrive at the boat of manifestation. It is all there for you, the poor little worm of the dust which has suddenly made its contact with the flesh-consciousness of which Jesus spoke.

The New Order is founded first on assumption. It has its beginnings in the recognition of the Word of Jesus Christ, and it moves on steadily, enlarging the borders of its tent and launching out into deeper waters.

Wrapped in secrecy after it has once discovered the Power, it "salutes no man" on the highway of life and religiously avoids the man "whose breath is in his nostrils"—the chatterbox who discusses and asks questions for the sake of debate and argument about God and salvation. There is no question the Higher Order of Beings needs to ask that cannot be answered by the inner Lord, whether it comes through his own or another's temple. He has the power of the full realization of "I will ask my Father," who is the supreme and only authority in the universe for giving the answer which exists before it is asked. You begin to sense-feel the way of Life in contradistinction to the old thought-taking processes.

Away with the feeble efforts of trying to make another believe you are spiritual! The spiritual hypocrite who strives to be acclaimed a demigod is in danger of the hellfire of exposure. There are not two lives—there is only One. There is not a spiritual life and another thing called a material life to the one who has made his *union*.

That there is nothing evil in Spirit's realm does not give license, but it doth give liberty and freedom of both thought and action.

After saying in one instance, "Ye ask ... that ye may consume it upon your lusts," the same Voice says, "Ask ... that your joy might be full ... heretofore you have asked for nothing." The two statements running side by side in the law make it seem a hodgepodge, a contradiction which the human thinker cannot check, and yet there is not a single contradiction or illogical statement in the whole Scriptures, if you know how to read.

This "advancing confidently" of which Thoreau speaks would seem to carry the thought of a serious business, of living a tight and narrow life. But there is nothing serious about Spirit. Spirit is joyous and gloriously free, unbound by anything that human wisdom—which is "foolishness in the eyes of God"—may set down for it; yet in this very freedom it has an integrity that is so amazingly meticulous that it makes the human sense of law seem as child's play.

The moment seriousness enters into the scene, we have heaviness, sacrifice, the mortifying of self, and all the other ugly things that belong to the erstwhile concept of the so-called saint. None of these unhappy things have anything to do with God. They are individual concepts of life. There is nothing in the law of Spirit that tells of them, and there is nothing in any of them that brings out the *joy* of which we are told Life consists.

There is ever a dearth of words to express the divine idea, and no man who still judges the word without the Spirit can afford to bother with the Christ teaching. "Awake thou that sleepest," and see the *Spirit of the word*, and then you will know that while seriousness cannot possibly enter into the law of Life, yet there is a balance, a poise, and an unfixed fixedness.

A child will be serious in his acceptance of Father Christmas, but he is not serious in the same way an adult would be if he were told about a comparably unusual occurrence in his life. Yet the child has all the essential integrity to make him fall into line with the most strict regulations of the legend, but with a joy and thrill and an acceptance that makes it all beautifully un-serious and glorious.

Do you begin to see that you cannot afford to be set and fixed in the revelation? The moment you have to "work" in the truth, you are working in the thought-concept of it. The acceptance of "I will" is far removed from the long line of affirmations and denials which you have been told are necessary to establish God here on earth. The more tense you become in the word of truth the less you accomplish, for it proves the less you believe in its indisputable reality.

There is nothing tense about nature bringing forth her luscious harvest. She literally pours herself into manifestation by the glorious unfolding of one stage after another.

So you, when you pray, "enter into your closet and shut the door, and the Father who seeth in secret shall reward thee openly." This very thing is what the tree does—if you must have an illustration. It retires into the very roots of itself and there remains in prayer, and soon it brings forth another glorious manifestation, proof that it has prayed aright—for it has prayed in the nature of itself. And that is what Jesus Christ said to you—pray in the *nature* name. For when you ask in the name-nature, your desire takes place for you in the easy, natural way.

It is wonderful when you begin to enter into this new order of things and become a resurrected being of Light. You do not care what people think or know— *you* know, and so let them pass; let them pass. In the name of Jesus Christ, put the seal on your lips and say no more about this deep secret until you are asked. Utter no word of argument nor listen to any. Why should you stand in the public place, casting pearls unto swine, who will only rend you because what you say is too good to be true and cannot be understood? Put the seal upon your lips. Never breathe a word about the inner soul of you or the workings of that soul until a direct demand is made on you. At that time you have the authority and the power to speak the Word that will bring about the desired change. Speak the Word—and let it rest.

The New Order to which you belong sense-knows things which cannot be put into words. It constantly appropriates more and more of the Presence by recognizing It and by magnifying It—asking the Father and calling forth the Word and knowing that *I* go before to prepare the way for you.

*I* go before to prepare the way for you—what do you think will happen when you recognize this as natural? You ask the Father and drop the whole thing.

You do not need to expect—you have accepted it and so it is. You keep your attention on the power of God Almighty and not on ways, means, etc.

It is wonderful. Praise God from whom all blessings flow. Do you hear? *All* blessings flow from God, and you cannot get blessings from any other source.

The New Order begins to make itself felt in you. You begin to read the Scriptures—see what a treasure chest it is for you, filled as it is with the ways of the *new* order of beings. Of course, it always has been so, just as everything has always existed but has not been recognized. So God always has been in all His fullness but has not been recognized. At first we recognized bits and parts of Him, but now we begin to take "the whole garment."

This New Order brings with it laws and things that cannot be uttered or written. They are above the language of humankind. It is glorious that you shall suddenly become conscious of yourself in the first person and present tense and begin to do the things that are divinely planned for you.

"The cattle on a thousand hills" are mine; if I am anhungered, I will "slay and eat." I will not have to ask. Do you hear this? I mean you—what will you do with it? Talk it over with another person and thresh all the Spirit out of it with words? Or will you sense-feel it and eat if you want to? If it is necessary to sustain the picture of harmony, you will appropriate the cattle.

All this lovely "advancing confidently" will not be for self-gratification or an enlarged ego, for when such a one sees the cattle on a thousand hills and kills one, he is arrested and thrown into prison, for the cattle did not belong to him, and he has violated human law and must be punished by human law.

It is glorious how divine law contradicts itself, one minute saying, "All that the Father hath is thine," and the next, telling you to work out your living "by the sweat of your brow." This is to throw dust into the eyes of the "wise" one who knows two powers, good and evil, and who, in reality, believes that the power of evil is stronger and surer than the power of God. It is wonderful how everything is withheld from that one; how he is tantalized with abundance all about him and yet cannot touch it. The sooner he begins to understand that Jesus Christ is a truthsayer and not a liar the sooner he will come into his Oneness, and there will be great rejoicing over this sinner, even as you and I are rejoiced in heaven (consciousness) when we come to the place of acknowledging Jesus Christ as the *Only*.

Let us return again to the words of the Spirit through Thoreau, as he tells of this new being who suddenly knows why he can go ahead confidently. "He will meet with a success unexpected." Yes, it is the unexpected thing that always happens, so don't expect anything. Keep that busy, human quality of expectation away from it all. You have already been given the perfect thing in Spirit; give this a moment in which to embody itself and become flesh. It can happen in the twinkling of the eye, if you will let it, by keeping yourself away from it. This lovely success of which man has never dreamed will come to him in "common hours"—just naturally and normally—not when he is making an effort, but in common hours, in just the ordinary hours of life.

"He will put something behind and pass an invisible boundary." Do you hear? You will pass an invisible boundary, the line of demarcation that the old human consciousness has set between matter and Spirit; and in passing this, man arrives at the Father-Consciousness.

Do you hear? Being of the New Order, you shall pass an invisible boundary. "I will go unto my Father" and "I will ask my Father." These are natural things. They are the passwords you take with you when you "go into expression" of anything—and in an instant you can cross the invisible boundary and enter into a place of *power* and *law,* which instantly disintegrates the most inexorable law of the human consciousness and sets things at such variance that the old Adam-thought, which is still heaping evil upon you, is dumfounded, confused, and put to shame; forced to say before this Power, "I am a liar, and the father of it."

Do you begin to see what Jesus Christ gave to us when He brought to our attention this Presence? And when He called it so simple a child could operate it and so natural that it just suddenly appeared, yet so "hidden from the wise and prudent" that they cannot find Me.

As you perceive this glorious heritage, you will expand in consciousness, appropriating more and more of it and entering more and more into the Secret Place, and you will "live with the license of a higher order of beings."

Yes, you will suddenly be enfolded in such a consciousness of the Presence that you will know what praying without ceasing means. It will give you the way of license in the true sense of the word, which is liberty and freedom and is above the curse of the law.

> It is this license that enables you to advance confidently into the consciousness which lies beyond the invisible boundary. I salute you.

# Chapter III

# Agreement

*Two shall agree as touching anything,*
*and it shall be established on the earth.*

In other words, it shall have a body and form. An invisible agreement shall be given a vehicle of expression.

This power of agreement is given to man. It is within the possibility of anybody who dares to understand and apply it. No matter what road you have traveled or how far awry you have gone, nor yet how befuddled you may be with strange teachings and people—every man has the power of agreement.

Agreement, in its truest interpretation, is *conception*. It is the thing which, when once accomplished, starts to fashion a body for the new idea. Once the conception has taken place, nothing can stay its manifestation—else the laws of God be false.

If you, for instance, could make an agreement in the truest sense of the word and then have the power to destroy that fulfillment—after the law precisely states that if two shall agree as touching anything on the earth it shall come to pass—then the whole teaching of Jesus Christ is in vain.

No, once you have "touched" and made the agreement, it will go on to fulfillment in spite of you. No matter then what doubt, fear, or even condemnation you may pour over the whole thing—that law of God must and will fulfill, whether you accept it or not.

One thing must be definitely established in your consciousness, and that is: "My words are spirit and my words are truth," and "they shall not return unto me void, but shall accomplish whereunto they are sent." And so you become better stabilized in life when you realize that you (even though through you this word or agreement has been spoken) cannot change or stay the on-going and the fulfillment of the Word. "Not one jot or tittle shall be removed until the word is fulfilled."

It is wonderful. It takes the whole matter out of the hands of your puny human-thinking apparatus, which would immediately attempt to set up a counter or negative word to destroy the Word of God.

If there is anything that can destroy the Word of God or the action of that Word, then it is high time we turned and worshiped that power, even though it be the devil, for we all know it is poor policy to be on the losing side.

Just what is your actual attitude toward the Word of God? Do you believe it? Do you know it? Do you know that it is something which is indivisible? The human mind uses millions of words in hundreds of languages to express the Word of God. But the Word of God is "the substance of all things hoped for" and the very "evidence of the things not seen."

Who are you or anybody else to handle the Word of God? It is depravity to imagine that a person, organization, or book has power apart from the *one Word of God*. And it is utter stupidity to imagine that the Word of God can be turned aside by any other power. The questioning, deceitful human thought throws a wall of opaque words in the way of the Word, and the human vision becomes so fore-shortened that it cannot see through the mist of its own wantonness and perceive the Christ every-where. "Having done all, stand" and "see the salvation of the Lord."

The time has come for actual living in the kingdom of heaven, and we are just around the corner from fulfillment, when the "things not seen" will be seen. Yet a little while—just a thorough house cleaning, as it were; a recapitulation of the actual Word of God in the midst of you.

Are you afraid to stand?

Don't stand like a martyr whining for release. Stand boldly on the recognition of the Word. Consign to hellfire all other beliefs and opinions. Are you yet questioning whether the Word of God is efficacious? Then you are still wishing and hoping, and nothing but disappointment will come to you.

Are you satisfied that the Word of God accomplishes, or do you secretly entertain the idea of fate, destiny, or some other power intervening? "Awake thou that sleepest, and Christ shall give thee light," and in the Light which shall emanate from the source of your being, you will be able to perceive the nothingness of all the lesser laws under which you have been operating and which have become strong and powerful by sustained thought.

When the agreement has been made, the conception takes place. From that moment, it is entirely out of your hands. I care not how negative and how doubtful you may be—not you or all your kind or the greatest authority on metaphysics can cause the Word of God to be turned aside.

Yes, I think you too will soon "arise and go unto my Father." I think you will soon see that the cleansing process which has been going on has been merely the getting rid of the great chaos caused by thought. All the dark forms and shadows which have stood in your path will disintegrate the moment you recognize this. They, together with all evil, are sustained and fed by thought. The moment your thought is taken from any of them, that moment the clay feet of the thought-created god begin to crumble, and its destruction is only a question of time.

"Who is so great a God as our God?" was the shout of the soul which had suddenly come out of its mesmeric state. Suddenly you will awake to this *oneness* of the Word. It fills all space, is in everything, and yet it remains whole and undivided. Changeless, too, so it comes not under the emotional, shifting ideas of the human mind.

All of us have gone into a far country. Even after we left Egypt, we were, and still are, capable of turning about and worshiping the gods of our fathers. Be not discouraged. Presently agreement will not be for the purpose of working a miracle but for the releasement of the Power into plainer manifestation.

"Two (you and another, you and your soul) shall agree as touching anything (that is a large measure—do you believe it possible?) and it shall be established on the earth." Can you take such a glorious law as possible? It cannot be accepted by the human mind, which knows that nothing is possible and which has proved over and over that even its best prayers are put to naught. You cannot accept God with the human mind because it is finite and cannot know the infinite. All this thought-taking process will fade away presently, and you will actually "be still, and know that I am God"—or else you will yet be arguing what "Mr. or Mrs. Blank" has to say on the subject.

There is only one Voice, and that is the Voice of the Christ-Consciousness in the midst of you. Either you listen to that Voice and live or you listen to the babble of voices and come tumbling down with the tower with which you attempted to reach heaven.

Heaven, to most people, is a multiplicity of "things." Yet without the proper perspective, these can become such a hell that they will crush one. Things are of no value in themselves. Value is placed upon things by man. The wise trader chuckles to himself because he has given the native islander a bolt of calico for a black pearl, but the value in both instances is placed by man. When you have the proper perspective of things (even money), you will know how it was possible for Jesus Christ to control the situation in which He found Himself.

You are a follower of Jesus Christ? See that you consult the source of your wisdom, and not some person. Whom do you follow? Whoever it is, you are going into a ditch from which you will have trouble getting out. All personality leads to the grave; the more you glorify it the sooner you will tumble headlong into the pit. "Awake thou that sleepest!" Many have already fallen into the pit of personality and are virtually dead. They are like whited sepulchers full of dead men's bones—full of the dead letter of some personality from whom they are trying to get the sustenance of life. "Awake thou that sleepest, and Christ shall give thee light"— awake and arise from the dead. It is wonderful, this coming out of the tomb of your own making.

Do not waste any more time whining over the evils that have been done to you by a personality. Rejoice that you are *awake,* even though you are yet sitting in the pit. "If ye be in the Spirit, ye are no more under the curse of the law." That ought to spring you out of any tomb, no matter how rock-walled it may be. "Get ye up unto a high mountain" —get up into the consciousness of the Presence, even though you are sitting in the filth of personal teaching.

"If two shall agree as touching anything, it shall be established on the earth." The agreement that accomplishes is made from the standpoint of pure recognition, and this recognition comes from the contemplation of the Power as *One*. No matter what the appearances at the time—they are as naught.

As you contemplate this Power as a definite reality, you begin to see some of the things which "eyes have not seen and ears have not heard" and to know some of the things which have not yet "entered into the heart of man" but which are already prepared for him.

One of these great things is the utter simplicity of it all—the overwhelming sense of power to transmute water into wine and to change the face of the earth (your earth). It is past finding out, past all understanding. It is so glorious and wonderful that it precipitates a thrilling paean of praise. Such a vibration of harmony sets in that the walls of a thousand Jerichos are shattered, and the way of the Lord is made plain and straight.

Do you begin to sense it? Do you begin to understand a little of the new dimension of which we are speaking? It has nothing to do with the old, outmoded thought-processes. It is pure and unadulterated inspiration that even at this instant is pouring through the temple of your being and is clearing out of the way all the manifestations of human thought.

Your temple is the body of Light, and nothing evil or untoward can remain after one moment's contemplation of the *All*-Presence.

"The word was made flesh and dwelt among them." This is the Word of agreement which you have *touched*, and it has now become flesh. Do not meddle with the gestation; do not bother with appearances. During this period, you will be cared for, if you do not get in the way with your human thought. Do you believe? Do you think this great universal Power can possibly do this impossible thing? Through the offices of your temple-being all things will be fulfilled, for your temple is the point where the New Idea is stepped down into visibility.

The Voice is again crying in the wilderness of human thought, asking that a way be prepared for the Lord.

Human thought, trying to model its ideas after the Divine, makes endless agreements and brings nothing but illegitimate ideas into the picture, distorted and twisted, or else lifeless — "clouds without rain." Thousands of seekers after the truth are so far on the outside and so hypnotized by human thought and appearances that they bring forth nothing but futile, lifeless shapes. Everything emanating from this source is a failure.

The agreement of which Jesus speaks is that which causes conception to take place and which is then entirely out of the hands of the individual. It will bring forth its immaculate child, which will rule its own path of expression perfectly and without hindrance or outside interference.

By now, even the most unlearned beginner on the path should know something about the advisability of silence. Your daily contemplation of the Power will not be through the human mind trying to "make" it stronger and stronger, but will be a magnifying of that which already is and which is changeless and which is already moving toward the fulfillment of your agreement.

An agreement goes out, as it were, and we might say describes a circle in which are gathered together all the negative, confused, and futile ideas the mind formerly held regarding the subject. It engulfs them little by little, or perhaps instantly, and when it has made the circle complete, it is as though a short circuit had taken place, and the entire field of human thought and its limitation regarding that particular situation is consumed with holy fire. Every bit of apparent life in any hindrance is electrocuted and finished. The moment it has made the circle, the agreement comes into being. The human thought regarding the situation then having been destroyed, nothing can or will keep it from coming into the flesh.

"Yet in my flesh shall I see God." Do you believe it? Then why not make this glorious agreement this moment; and from the instant you have released it with pure recognition, stand and magnify the Lord, and the way of its coming into being shall be beautiful and glorious.

A new step in the revelation of the Truth is taking place. We are eliminating more and more of the apparent laws of human thinking. Look back for a moment and see the amusing little things you considered obstacles years ago. Today you are working at the roots of such things as human destiny, fate—laws so time-honored and hoary with age and "proof" that they seemed impossible to change. But when they are approached individually from the standpoint of the Christ-Consciousness, they are proved to be mere paper maché creations of human history. Every time you magnify the Power in the midst of you and in the midst of all things, you are undermining some false god. You are attempting things now that you formerly did not even consider as possible.

Time was, when you were satisfied to have a pretty affirmation on a card, decorated with scrolls and roses, and thought because you repeated this twenty times you could and would change something. You know differently now. You know that "taking thought" will get you nowhere, and while it may seem a little difficult to cut through at the moment, yet will your contemplation of the Presence begin to show you new dimensions that cannot be put into words or written on paper.

"Be still!" Do you hear? "Be still." There are many things to be said to you which will cause your heart to thrill with joy. You will say inwardly and outwardly, "I *know* that my Redeemer liveth." If He liveth, then your life is secure and expressing in the way of harmony.

Do you believe that *God is?* Answer me. Ye have come to the place of the absolute acknowledgment, the contemplation of the Presence and Power. It is wonderful. Praise God from whom all blessings flow. Or have you another source? A person, a job, or an organization? Answer all these question for yourself.

This great awakening out of the thought-taking process is pushing on to the deeper things of which Jesus spoke. *Even unto the last enemy.*

Now "two shall agree as touching anything, and it shall be established on the earth."

Do you see a little about the idea of agreement? The agreement backed up by the consciousness that "My words are power, and they are Spirit, and they shall not return unto Me void, but shall accomplish whereunto they are sent." It thrills one to know that all this lovely process is entirely beyond the interference of the human mind with its opinions and tried-and-true laws.

> The captive is going free, for his prison walls
> of thought are crumbling even now. Even now,
> you have found a ransom. You are beginning to
> *see.*

# Chapter IV

# Life Eternal

"This is life eternal" — to know Me. The moment we touch the thing called *eternal*, we are beyond the bounds of all temporal things and that which goes with them — sin, disease, and death. It is as if a man were imprisoned in a circle of his personality, hedged about with all the events of human life, from which there was no escape. He might travel away from any disagreeable event found in the circumference, to the center of his being or circle, but the moment he came out from that center again, he would meet a host of other evils which would envelop him. He could plunge into the center of his being and find a temporary surcease from the evils of his personality, but all the while the clock of events would be bringing him to one terrible and inevitable thing — uncertainty, death, and oblivion.

The futility of the human pattern is too great to contemplate. If a man stops for a moment to reflect on the hopelessness of it, he loses his mental balance, finding himself in a situation not unlike a beetle in a slippery glass bowl, by Herculean efforts pulling himself up a little toward the rim of his prison, only to slip back to the bottom again. And this practice goes on until he has spent the last ounce of energy — and dies.

Jesus, the carpenter, came with the consciousness of immortality, the consciousness that resident in every man is the place, or point of contact, with the Oversoul—that permanent identity called *Father*—which, if a man ever established and reached, would initiate him into the Fatherhood degree of life and would cause him to begin the "Life Eternal" cycle of his being. It is so illusive and intangible that the moment clumsy human thinking approaches it, it has apparently fled. The Spirit is like the wind—it "bloweth where it listeth, and no man knoweth whither it cometh or whither it goeth." So is it with this new, intangible truth.

Man, the human concept, with his limitations of thought, bumps into a solid, immovable wall made up of pairs of opposites—good and bad, sickness and health, riches and poverty, etc. Finally, in a state of desperation, he turns from this futility and, self-hypnotized, takes up what he calls a "battle" against evil—and is surprisingly happy if, after praying terrifically to a God he proclaims as All-Present, he is able to manifest just enough to live on.

It is amazing to what degree the self-hypnotism extends. We have become so used to it that we actually stand and give thanks for the problems of life. It is a tragic situation to give thanks for evil because there is no other way to dispose of it. To acknowledge a definite power of evil which is stronger than good, he cannot do and live, so he hypnotizes himself to the actual facts of life and "fights a good fight" yet claims to be following after a man two thousand years ago who said, "Call not me good," and, "Ye do not need to fight."

When Truth is presented to the world, it is nude, stripped of every rag of belief, and for this reason it blinds the eyes of man, who has been hiding behind the thick veil of beliefs. He protests that he is being humiliated; he uses any excuse to cover the shining Presence with clothes of his own making. He slips over It a gaudy robe of sleazy human opinions and ideas— and copyrights God.

Hence, God is turned into a system. We have the Blank system of God and the So-and-So system of God— both of which oppose each other and both of which claim to be the only way; both of which are dredged by the lusty, gluttonous soul of some individual. All this is within the prescribed circle of human thought. But "this is life eternal, to know Me" still thunders on the diaphragm of consciousness. Man knows that somewhere there is a release, but it is always thought to be outside himself. Or if inside, it is inside his *personality* and never within Himself—Him, He, Father.

This eternality cannot be demonstrated by thinking about it anymore than healings can be made that way. It is true that many manifestations of willpower are brought temporarily into being, but the moment the willpower diminishes—as it must—so does the manifestation. There is nothing that can possibly be healed in God, and the declaration that God is *all* Presence,

45

followed by an attempt to establish even a belief in disease, shows the chaos of the human mind.

It is true, symbolically, that you have performed the Adam and Eve experience and have been driven (self-driven) out of your divine Consciousness of Me into the wilderness of three-dimensional thinking wherein all things are distorted, and evil, ruin, and death are the definite ends.

The Bible is full of invitations into this next dimension of life. "Come unto me, all ye that labor and are heavy laden, and I will give you rest." Do you begin to sense something which cannot be done by thought? It is done through the conscious recognition of the facts of life and through the appropriation of your status of Fatherhood.

"At a moment ye think not, I come"—a serene recognition that I AM THAT I AM has sent me into expression—without waiting for the signs, which are to follow as soon as signs cease to be necessary. As soon as manifestation is natural, normal, and automatic, then will you neutralize all the terrible mental harangue about life on the three-dimensional plane.

There will be a quieting of all the questing for signs, a divine indifference, because suddenly you have found *Him*, the very Fatherhood of you, and from that point on, you are functioning on a different plane. You no more look up to, but out upon, the finished mystery. What you then "tell the Father in secret" is proclaimed from the housetops of manifestation.

You are no more the child begging for the toy. You are one with the Father, giving and supplying, through revelation, that which eternally is. Such waves and waves of light-consciousness pass over you that eventually these floods of Spirit will wash out the cells of your temple, and all the "former things will have passed away," for the memory of such human events as age, unhappiness, sin, and death are all held in place and sustained by conscious thinking and by looking at the records of memory—the subconscious mind.

Presently all the kinks and distorted outlines of this manifestation, which you have created through your evil thinking, are lost. "If you lose your life, ye shall find it"—a paradoxical statement meaning precisely nothing and yet revealing the Way, the Truth, and the Light by which you shall enter into your heritage and be saved from the evil of human thinking. "Behold, I make all things new,"—fresh, lovely, beyond the trifling history and records of your "John Smith."

Behold! I make all things new. Do you begin to *sense* the Presence, the shining Presence which says to you, "This is life eternal, to know Me," the Me of your divinity that is waiting for you suddenly to "go in and possess the land" instead of begging for a sign?

No further signs will be given you; already you have had many of them. Now when you ask for further signs, you find yourself in the desert of waiting, and no signs are given. The man who multiplied the bread and the fishes yesterday has mysteriously disappeared, and you are walking in the hot desert of trying to get something for nothing—which becomes the cursed Desert of Waiting—until the blistering sun of human knowledge says to you, "Well, there was nothing to it anyway; it never did happen; or if it did, it was only a coincidence." And it also says, "There is another man over in another city; he is making bread and making money. Let's go over there and learn his secret."

With the mock humility of worshiper, you approach him, willing to ingratiate yourself to the lowest degree on the outside in order to wrench from him the secret. He lets you crawl like a dog under the table, knowing full well what you are after. Soon you are out again after another teacher, and so the circus goes on until you arise in the integrity of your Christ-given authority and enter into the heritage of "this is life eternal, to know Me," and you find it all there—everything that you sought and everything that you tried to demonstrate and more—for "eyes have not seen and ears have not heard, neither has it entered into the heart of man, the things that are prepared for those that love the law (Lord)."

"O taste and see that the Lord is good." Such a glorious awakening from the filthy dream of life in the body of sin, disease, and death, into the glorious revelation of the Shining Presence in the midst of you here and now.

"Who did hinder ye that ye should not obey the truth?" "Why, I did, Lord." Suddenly I have discovered where all the hindrance lay. I had thought it was this one or that one or this or that condition, but suddenly — ah, suddenly I find that I have hindered myself. And it would be sad, indeed, to discover this if I still had to remain under the law of mortality and death. But at the moment of my discovery of what was hindering me, I also discovered the immortality of Me, and I sensed, if only in a slight way, what it means to *"know Me."*

It is as if one were suddenly swept up from the earth in a huge airplane. Quickly people become mere ants, running about meaninglessly on the ground. Then the houses fade from view, and the whole landscape becomes a huge colored map. All your problems that lay there are submerged — they cannot find you — and if you remain in this Presence long enough, consciously, when you return to the ground, "the place thereof is no more."

To be lifted up into this Fatherhood state of your being is automatically to dissolve a thousand and one annoying circumstances over which you have spent endless time in an effort to solve. It is an automatic release from the hard-fast indentations of human thought.

Anything is possible in this state of "if I be lifted up." If I am lifted up to the I AM Fatherhood degree within every man, I shall then be able to perceive the perfect picture "shown to me on the mount," and on this mount of transfiguration — where the mutable is made immutable, the unreal, real — the hard-fast patterns of human thinking, history, and "proof" are dissolved and reduced to their primal nothingness again. Then the perfect picture becomes a pattern in consciousness so that when you return to the manifest state of things, behold, all things are changed—all things are made new.

It is something so beyond the words I am using to describe it that it comes under the head of pure, unadulterated revelation. The more we try to handle it with human thought the more it recedes from the realm of possibility, and finally it seems to have been but a dream in the night.

This appearing and disappearing will continue until the consciousness of the Presence is so natural and well-established within you that the thing called miracle will become the thing called natural; for it is a seeing with the "look again" dimension—past all the time-space-and-belief thought-walls erected by the best wisdom of man. It is all so sacred and holy that it is beyond consideration by the vulgar eyes of the one who is trying to demonstrate things, when you are in the very Sea of Substance and can bring into being that which you see as already prepared.

> It is wonderful—floods of light are passing through the consciousness; white light which, when it is passed through the desires of your heart, is broken up into a multicolored variety of manifestation.

Just as white light is invisible and contains all the colors of the spectrum just so do you find in this invisible power of the Presence that "all things, whatsoever you ask," are there before you ask. And so it is most necessary to establish, once and for always, the presence of the White Light.

Human thought is after the various manifestations. No sooner does it grasp one of them than it disintegrates, just as money passes through the fingers of the uninitiate. But the seeking and finding of the White Light of the Presence as the very source of the All furnishes a constant stream of manifestation, from the unseen through into the things that can be seen and are handled by human hands.

It is wonderful. The New Day is dawning, the new age—the age of "yea, yea" and "nay, nay," the time when all argument pro and con is finished in favor of the *isness* of the Presence in which is the fullness of all things.

"Whatsoever you ask in my nature"—whatsoever you then ask, whatever "color" you choose to draw into materialization, can be done because of the conscious recognition of the Presence of the White Light, which is filled with the *All* of creation.

All effort to establish the stupid idea that human belief in its highest and most powerful form can cheat and harm and hurt the Father degree of consciousness is utter foolishness, for though it apparently be master of the situation, with such proof as to make a strong man quail, yet by reason of this recognition of the Shining Presence in which you live, move, and have your being, will everything be adjusted, and not one jot or tittle be lost when the law is fulfilled.

You can, therefore, lose nothing, never have lost anything. In the twinkling of an eye, the whole mortal thought-universe of evil, with its crooked ways and means, is put to flight—but before it flees it must bless you with a complete and absolute release. "The years that the locusts have eaten are restored." As soon as you see this, all years that the locusts of human thought have taken from you shall be restored because you are moving into immortality and are beginning to sense the new dimension of life.

*This* (right here and now) is life eternal—to know your Fatherhood degree of life. This is the day of salvation and the day of forgetfulness of the former things, laws, beliefs, evils, etc. It is the day of revelation and manifestation. You are even now moving in the flood of this new Light. The Father is coming toward you, even as He moved toward the Prodigal when the Prodigal arose and turned in the direction of the Father. As soon as he "recognized the Father" he arose, and at that moment the Father sym- ... etc.

It is all in the truth for you—this meeting between you and the Father and this business of finally being absorbed into the immortality of your Fatherhood degree of life.

# Chapter V

# I Am the Light

*I am the light of the world …*

… A light that "shineth in darkness, and the darkness comprehendeth it not." So is it with the I AM of you. Once discovered and identified as *you*, it brings a Light unto this world of human thought-taking shadows. *The moment this is established, you will begin to experience the automatic effect of light on darkness.* You have for ages been trying to "bring" the light from some outside region—either up (in heaven) or from some far-away place of mystery. From time to time, you have apparently been able to do just this. But your success was so fleeting and irregular that it came under the heading of "miracle."

Yet "I am the light of the world" stands, and until you discover and identify yourself with your I AM— the Father to whom Jesus immediately turned and associated Himself in Oneness—you will not be able to dispel much of the human-thinking darkness which you have drawn to yourself. It is wonderful when the revelation of your Permanent Identity breaks over you. It is this identification with the Father, "I and my Father are one," that gave Jesus Christ the power over the shadows of His Jesus-consciousness. It was this nearness and naturalness of the Father within that made Him what He was; and it is this same consciousness which will change you and cause wonders to happen—miracles to the thought-clogged mentalities about you, but to you just revelations from the standpoint of your new plane of consciousness.

The attempt to establish this new revelation is, of course, fraught with the limitation of a language which is three-dimensional and is trying to "utter the unutterable Word." Yet by arranging its utterable words in inspired patterns, suddenly the unwritten or unuttered Word becomes real.

But first and above all, the question asked a hundred times in these pages, "believest thou this?" must be answered by you. If, to the teachings of Jesus in their entirety, you cannot answer in the affirmative, then you are holding a reservation for some other than God Almighty and have not yet recognized Him *supreme*. It is futile to imagine that you can deny this omnipotence and hope to attain results with a divided allegiance. It is all or nothing. And it cannot be *all* on the three-dimensional, thought-taking plane on which we found ourselves when Jesus Christ first came.

"If you deny me, I shall also deny you" is quite normal reaction. When you throw a rubber ball against a wall, it returns to you with the force with which it was thrown. You are not surprised. If you deny the power of Jesus Christ as a reality, then when you call upon it, nothing responds, for you have already established the consciousness which does not believe in it and are only saying words. Be not like the heathen, who think by repeating many words to gain the ear of God. There is only *one Word*, and the moment that is felt-uttered, It breaks itself up into thousands of human words, depending upon the language in which you think.

A man may think in any language or several, but he only "feels" in one, the unspoken language of the heart-soul. So the universal language is the urge or sensing quality. The moment it is accepted in recognition, it is able to say, "I believe," for it is not measuring by anything found in human consciousness.

It is wonderful when this becomes true to you, for the moment it does, you begin to *know* in the right sense of the word. It is not a "think-knowing," but a "feel-knowing," and this is not emotional or sentimental. It is something so well balanced and so free from all the sensations of the think-knowing as to be free from any curiosity or questioning. When this "feel-know" is touched, the manifestation will follow, either instantly or later—but at the precise moment when it should.

Imagine the cripple at the temple gate, ever dreaming of suddenly leaping and dancing, free and in perfect bodily condition. He could have been able to think about it only as the "impossible," yet it took place—and mark you, he had no time to study any system of Truth or hear any dissertations on the subject. He was able to believe, or accept the gift, and the Father within answered for him, "Yea, Lord," in agreement and came forth with full capacity to do that which he was called upon to do.

The only reason anything can ever take place in you is because the Father-Consciousness within you has full capacity to accomplish it. Otherwise there would be no manifest results. If this Father-Consciousness were not already there, you could not implant it there by any amount of thinking, for it is entirely too fantastic for human thought to handle.

You see, then, we are not trying to bring something new to you; not asking you to create a new consciousness or to do something. We are merely calling attention to that which actually exists in you and has always existed in you. It was through the discovery of this that Jesus, the carpenter, was able to do things that "Jesus, the Carpenter" could not do, yet did. Whatever has been accomplished, at any time, above the line of human thinking has been done through this same discovery, in a degree.

True, this Father may be buried beneath centuries of human thinking, intelligence, and findings. He may be covered with the deep incrustation of "I have never seen it done, nor have I ever known any who has seen it done," and to extricate the Father from this morass of beliefs seems a labor for a spiritual Hercules. If he approaches it through the limitation of the material, he finds his Augean Stables too much for him and gives up in despair.

Perhaps he then starts a long and tiresome study of it all, and yet—remember the wretch at the temple gate, with a life filled with evil, suddenly releasing this Father? It thrills one to think that instead of all this human palsy-like movement of thought, the cripple was suddenly freed, and the entire manifestation of evil absorbed, transformed. The old body was not destroyed or gotten rid of, but the union of Father and Son released the perfect manifestation.

Can you believe? Well, not until this "I am the light of the world" becomes *you*; until in a natural, normal state of mind, you are able to accept this wonderful revelation. Over and over again, you "try" to do this—but presently you *see* what it is, and then you dare to call upon the Father as naturally as you would call upon your human father, were he in the next room. What would he do if you called upon him in the day of trouble? He would rush to help you in every possible way. So just as you know this to be natural (it is what you and everybody else would expect) so must this calling on the Father within be natural, normal, and easy. I must stress to you that it is *easy* and *natural* and *normal*. You must not make an event of it.

Instantly, when Jesus (the carpenter) called upon His Father, He (Jesus) became Jesus Christ—"one with the Father." And this elevation caused the Light to shine in the darkness, to illumine the human situation and reveal the nothingness of the mortal or matter thinking-pictures. So powerful is this Light that no combination of laws, thoughts, or opinions can or will stand against it. In the case of the cripple, we see it wiping out forty years of accumulated belief with the same ease as it might have brushed away a single thought. Do you believe? You cannot believe it with the human thought-taking process, for it is utterly impossible.

There is "so much to do" in your present situation before it is ready to manifest the new state of things that your poor mind is worn out trying to "dream" about it all. If you do not watch, you will find yourself saying, "Well, when I come (on earth) again, I will do so and so." When you come again, you come with all the limitations you take with you, for the experience of dropping off the body does not suddenly enlighten you.

You remark how natural it all was to Jesus, and the human mind says, as an excuse for its failure to experience fulfillment, health, and joy here and *now*, "Oh, yes, but that was Jesus, and He had a special power," and so you will set up a Jesus, against His own admonition: "Call not me good." Do not mistake who "doeth the works— "Call not me good." And in further defense of the revelation, He made it plain that anything He had ever done, and even greater works, were possible to *you*. Do you believe? You must answer this yourself.

We have seen that the cripple did not have time to think about his problem—he had been doing that for forty years—but suddenly he was able to believe, and in that one instant, "in the twinkling of an eye," was he able to change his entire bodily manifestation. Yet all that took place was a showing forth of that which had always existed. It was that which had been created "in the beginning," perfect and eternal in the heavens.

It is wonderful. It makes your situation so possible of change. You are suddenly released from a straitjacket of human thinking, which has bound you and crippled your capacities. No body could of itself be crippled or ugly or aged. It must have over it a bondage of hateful human thinking which, like unto many ropes and chains, cut deep into the flesh and fester in ugliness and discord. Break any of these cords or ropes of human thought, and it experiences what the world calls a healing, but it is only an aperture through which the Light has come into being.

All this seems vague and hypothetical; yet in reality, the moment the thought-force is taken away from anything, that thing comes to its natural form and shape again, just as a soft rubber ball crushed in the hands will return to its normal, perfect symmetry the moment the fingers have released it.

> Break the thought on a given problem and the abnormal manifestations of that problem go out of the picture.

Where do they go? The force that was formerly used to hold them in place is absorbed and picked up, and the moment this occurs, the manifestation which was sustained by this force drops out of sight.

So you begin to see what it is to "be still, and know that I am God" and why Paul, in an impassioned moment, when he had cut through to this *Oneness*, literally screamed, "Know ye not that ye are gods," trying to bring to the Greeks (who understand so well the "gods" and their alleged unlimited powers) just what it must mean to know what "Jesus" was revealing to the world. "Know ye not that ye are gods?" was some question to ask the ancient Greeks, who believed so strongly in the powers of their gods.

When Jesus asks you, "Believest thou this?" you are confronted by the same thing. Do you believe it is possible for you to do the works that He did and even greater works? In other words, do you believe that you are gods? Many human minds have tried it and thought to set up a human god, only to have him fall in due season with all the trademarked trappings of his reign. Yet the question stands. Will you do the works of Jesus Christ? Or will you still parry the question and make what you think are modest excuses?

Are you afraid, or do you still want to "save your darling (personality) from the flames" of Life which will consume it in order that your Permanent Identity may be made manifest?

It is wonderful when you begin to glimpse this Father-within consciousness as natural, normal, and easy and dare to call upon Me and instantly experience the change which the Light brings to the shadowy valley of thought in which you have been living all these centuries.

The coming of light to a shadow-world does no overcoming or setting aside of realities. What seemed so real and impossible to the shadow kingdom is no problem to the Light.

For instance, if it were possible for you to enter a two-dimensional kingdom and see it working, it would be one of length and breadth with no height, and everything would have to take place flat on the ground. Circumscribing a shadow with a square of darkness would not constitute any problem for you, but if the shadow-being had consciousness of it, he would know this to be a wall over which he could not climb, and he would have a problem. This problem would be as real to him as yours is to you.

Then, entering this present kingdom with its consciousness of the third dimension, height, would instantly make nothing of all the problems of the two-dimensional. A wall of shadow is nothing to you. You will glibly say, "It only *seems* to be a wall." But to the two-dimensional being, it is solid, made of the same substance of which he is composed, and has the same power to him as a wall of matter has to you. But you find a wall of shadow nothing. You use no force or effort on it, nor do you try to suggest ways and means of overcoming it.

While the shadowy being complains of its reality, you are not concerned with its (to him) awful manifestation. But there is no way for this other to escape his prison except he enters the third dimension. The moment he does this, he too sees his prison nothing but a shadow and smilingly walks through it. It has no bondage for him now.

Thus, when Jesus came to your world, He found you bound by many prisons, all of them as imaginary and unreal as the shadowy wall to the shadow man. Yet even as the latter protested about the reality of his condition, so do you spend your entire life trying to overcome matter with matter. You can picture a wall so solid that nothing can penetrate it and can back this up by the testimony of the entire race of your world. You can argue and wonder and speculate.

Unless you accept the revelation of Jesus Christ and enter into the new consciousness (dimension), there is little you can do to stave off the oncoming destruction which rushes toward every human. He has no escape through matter, for from the moment he arrives on the scene of the human drama, he is warned about the awful onslaught of evil rampant in the world. He has no chance. He may steal a few hours of joy out of the hell of it all, but he knows so many laws of reaction to everything good that he is filled with fear, the while he is snatching his stolen hours of happiness.

Jesus came, aware of this benignant Father within. So conscious was He of Him and His power that He went through every form of evil, to prove vicariously to you that in the Father realm any so-called human problem is as nothing—just as you might have placed yourself inside the shadow-ring prison and then walked through the walls or gone over to "the other side of the lake" or done anything to prove to those fearful shadow-beings that there was nothing to fear and no further need to remain in the limitation consciousness.

So Jesus, with His wonderful revelation, said that in the dimension of the Father-within consciousness there is no problem and what we call sickness, sin, death, are not real—and proceeded to show them as untrue and powerless to touch you, the moment you arise and take off from the level of the Father-within consciousness.

Then the beautiful statement, "I and my Father are one." But lest you might mistake this and make yourself a high priest or priestess, setting your personal self up as a demigod, He added, "My Father is greater than I." The universal Father-God is greater than the point (flesh) through which It expresses.

Do you begin to understand that the combination of you and your Father within causes you to be a perfect "stepper-down" of the universal God-power? Do you grasp how it was that Jesus quite naturally and calmly said, "I will ask my Father," and always had the answer before He asked? Or is it still baffling to the three-dimensional consciousness, which tries to measure this new dimension through the limitation of old beliefs?

"I will ask my Father," and so will you begin to do this very thing. First, you will recognize that you have a Father—before this, you will acknowledge there is a God universally present, and then you will see the need for understanding that you can no longer glorify yourself. *I* must increase, you must decrease. If you are out to make a name as a great teacher or healer, you are going to be disappointed, for you are still trying to glorify the old three-dimensional man. Do you think being spiritual will be any novelty to you in this New Day? It is only a curiosity to those who still think it some unique gift to a favored few. Who are you? When do you want to be *nothing* so that you can be everything? Answer me.

You may *have to* be great and famous and all that. I said *have to*, and how perfectly Jesus understood that. He was famous—not for Jesus, but that the salvation of the Lord might be revealed to mankind.

Do you begin to see what this wonderful revelation is about? You, in your New Day, naturally, normally, easily taking possession of your own kingdom and then being silent about it and letting your light shine for the glorification of God, automatically. You *are* the light the moment you and your Father are *one*, and you bring the light with you and dispel many shadowy prisons that you know nothing about. You are not trying to "do good."

You become conscious of this wonder, "I and my Father are one," and for that reason, anything is possible to you. You may touch, taste, see, hear—yes, even smell this glorious revelation into manifestation.

*Well, you can if you can.* You know whether you can or not. It may be too utterly difficult to you, but that is all right. The child can do it. How would you like to exchange places with him? Appropriate his consciousness? Can you? Or can you. And if not, what great lump of human importance is blocking your way?

Who would not bend the knee to the name *Jesus* out of sheer love of a human character, who might have followed the old, old pattern of keeping a modicum of this power for Himself. How easily He could have glorified Himself with a new system of teaching, trademarking it and flanking it about with man-made ideas of what must be done. Is this character not lovely, altogether lovely? And does it not make the hypocrites, who invent ways and means under a John Smith name whereby the Word of God may be measured out to mankind, seem despicable and shoddy?

And who, then, cannot put the burning coal of fire (which sears the last vestige of separation and human sense out of your life and closes once and for all time the door of your mouth to all chattering of and about the Word) on his lips? This coal of fire which seals your ears to all argument and proof of evil.

The Jesus Christ Consciousness is to you a lovely dawn of the New Day.

The never-ending source of inspiration pours through you, and you do not have to go back to get anything from the land of Sodom and Gomorrah. Nothing is there which you need or want—nothing of any value.

The light that "shineth in darkness and the darkness comprehendeth it not" is your light, and it makes no difference whether the darkness comprehendeth it or not. That is of no importance to you.

"My ways are past finding out"—so it is well.
"Know ye not that ye are gods?"

# Chapter VI

# By My Spirit

*Not by might, nor by power,*
*but by my spirit, saith the Lord.*

It is not by trying or forcing, nor yet by doing nothing and waiting for the manifestation that it comes into being, but by My Spirit. By the Spirit which moves on the face of the deep and reveals that which is hidden therein. It is by the recognition of this Presence so completely that to call upon Me is to have the answer. "Before they call, I will answer."

It is all too divinely subtle to human reasoning, with its thickened hearing and its dim sight. It cannot see nor yet hear what the Scriptures say unto the churches (bodies)—unto you. What the Spirit is saying to *you* and what you desire of all things to hear cannot come by force, power, or might, *but through Spirit.*

It is maddening to the human intellect to have such a thing said to it; just as it is not understandable to hear, "Take no thought of the body, what ye shall wear," etc. For the business of the human mind is taking thought and holding thought and working with thought, in spite of the admonition to "take no thought."

How is it that "a house divided against itself shall fall?" Because you cannot profess to follow after

Jesus Christ and then go against one of the foremost laws laid down by Him: "Take no thought for the scrip, the journey, the purse, the upper chamber, the ring, the robe," etc., etc., ad infinitum.

"Well then, what do I do?" You do as the Master told you to do—believe. And this believing has nothing to do with wishing, hoping, affirming, or "knowing the truth." It is a state of consciousness which is able to accept that which the human mind finds impossible. It can do this with certainty only when it has stopped looking for a sign. No more signs will be given—if you want your blessings, you have to believe without the sign.

This should not be difficult when you remember that you have made a colossal failure in the human way of achievement. So it should not be hard for you to completely give over and *let* the Light and the mind be in you which were also in Christ Jesus, since everything you have "tried" to do has gone awry.

When once, through the acceptance of the simple teaching of Jesus Christ, you have come to the "believe" state of things, then do you experience "the inspiration of the Almighty," which shall lead you into all things. Do you believe this? Not by your human thinking, for there is no way you can teach or learn inspiration—the quality of Life that suddenly makes itself manifest in you when you have come to accept the Presence as here and now. It is the "quickening" influence that is yours—and you are aware of it all suddenly.

This will make a success of whatever you are doing, no matter in what degree it is at present. If you are already successful, it will make you more so because it takes away all fear and all guessing about life, and promotes something in your work which causes it to be uniquely original and individual and automatically draws to you manifestation from every direction.

Do you begin to see why it is not by might nor power, but by My spirit that things are brought to pass that could not come to pass?

The more natural the words and works of Jesus Christ become to you, the more you will enlarge the borders of your tent and launch out into deeper waters; the more you will push out into new fields of manifestation. You will dare, do, and "be silent" in a new way, for now you are not trying to impress anyone that you are a great spiritual light. If you are such, it will be seen without your efforts.

The whole thing takes place within you, and *there* is also the place of accounting. Nothing can be lost or misappropriated in this place of the Father. You will get full credit and wages for all that you do. As the laborer, you are "worthy of your hire." Since this is a law, nothing any man can do can take it from you. Nothing that any organization or false belief attempts to establish shall keep from you that which is yours, and you will not bother about appearances, for once you have performed it in consciousness, it is yours in manifestation.

The more you turn to the Father within and acknowledge your Oneness and magnify the Lord, the more you will see your desires coming into being by a way you knew not of. "Heaven and earth are full of thee." And "thee" is all that you need. If it is full of *thee* ("the substance of things hoped for, the evidence of things not seen"), you will understand why it is so essential for you to recognize the Presence.

The more you (mortal) decrease, the more *I* (Spirit) will increase; and the more the power of the Father will be felt guiding the affairs of the temple, or Jesus, until finally the two are completely *One*, and then the will of God is being done, which means a life of constant harmony and joy, filled with the surprises that keep it fresh and new and possessed of an endless variety of expression. Believest thou this?

Do you begin to understand that the way of manifestation is not by might, nor by power, but by My spirit? The more natural this becomes to you the more you will expand into new fields of activity— and find the answer before the question and perceive that the inspiration of the Almighty is yours to draw upon at a moment's notice and whenever it is necessary to "step up" the powerless human consciousness. The moment you accept these great truths as real, natural, and eternal, that moment you begin to experience a new setup in your daily life. For this "inspiration of the Almighty" will lead you into *all* things— and all is enough.

Do you hear? It says *all* things — not some things, but *all* things, whatsoever you will? Do you believe? Can you believe? It is so wonderful what happens by this simple truth as given by Jesus Christ.

The leaven has already entered the three measures of meal, and the change is taking place *now*. Little by little, the whole substance is changed into leaven, and then it is changed again into bread. So is it with you. The Word of God has already descended into the stagnant pool of your human thought and has troubled the waters and started the change of base necessary for the new rate of vibration, of Spirit, to express. It is, in a way, like unto changing electrical equipment in order that greater watt power may be released.

You cannot graft holiness onto unholiness; neither can you force the fine subtle substance of Spirit through the opaque consciousness which is entirely unsuited to express or understand it. "Ye must be born again" is the only possible solution, and this borning again is actually taking place in you at this moment.

A new instrument of receptivity is being developed within you, a new consciousness which says, in reality, "Whereas before I was blind, now I can see." See what? See what has always been there to see but which could not be perceived by the human consciousness — just as the human consciousness, with its laws of physics, cannot see how a heavier-than-water body can possibly walk on the water and how an inflammable thing like flesh can walk through flames and not be burned. It has nothing in its mental makeup with which to understand these things and quite naturally comes to the conclusion that they are impossible — and so they are, to that state of consciousness.

Jesus explained them when He said, "I can of myself do nothing." It is wonderful how the Light is gradually coming through—that you must put on the "incorruptible," the new consciousness, if you expect to appropriate the gifts of Spirit.

Remembering again that all this is possible to the child, do not become involved with some method of making this appropriation. It needs only acceptance. As soon as the recognition or the acceptance takes place, the fertile egg is under the hen, and nothing can keep it from coming into its new state of consciousness unless the warmth of the mother bird be taken from it.

So is it with you; so was it with Mary. She magnified the Lord within her, and the development took place along natural and normal lines. Your part in bringing out this new recognition is to cease once and for always looking for results or examining into the development and to keep the attention on "magnifying the Lord within you."

You see, then, how utterly impossible it is to continue to live at the level of mental demonstrations, working with the human consciousness. You see also the need for secrecy in the new manifestation, for no one "whose breath is in his nostrils" will believe you.

It is "by my spirit," by the Spirit of this Lord, that the unexplainable change or transmutation takes place. It is not by power, nor by might. It is not by argument or by working with thought-forms called matter. It is not by trying to overcome fire that you walk through fire. It is because you have recognized a degree of Spirit which is not affected by fire.

And so will it be along all the other phases of your life. You will finally see that the consciousness into which you are moving is not an overcomer in any sense of the word. It is a degree above the condition and therefore has dominion over the condition. *It is not at war with the condition.*

So with the consciousness of prosperity. It is not at war with a belief in poverty. It is not fighting a lack nor yet a sense of lack, for in this new place of expression there is nothing to be desired. It is just so, and no matter how many times the manifestation may be swept away, it will replace itself because it is eternally in consciousness.

The manifestation of substance takes place, then, with ease and naturalness, and it does not thrill you in the sense that you have done something difficult or something unique. It is more and more understood as the natural thing to take place. Anything that attempts to prevent the sense of continued harmony in the realm of the manifest is disseminated by this Spirit and not by might or by power. It is the wholesale acceptance of this Jesus Christ that causes you to see the change that is even now going on within you —a blessed new estate where the former things are passed away and shall not be remembered nor come into mind any more.

So into the world—your world—you go to preach the gospel. You come into it with this new consciousness which is not going to destroy, but fulfill—yet this very fulfilling actually does destroy the limitations of the former consciousness. But you come into your world silently and easily, and everything you contact, if it but *touch* you, will be healed and made whole because you have stopped "using" the Spirit of the Lord. You *are* that Spirit, and any thing or body who recognizes this can and will receive the Light therefrom. They may not, in many instances, do it consciously. From a conscious standpoint, they may not know it has taken place at the moment, and from the human sense of things you may not get credit —which is a grand thing to know, because you do not need credit from the outside. All that is taken care of from within.

You may literally touch some one who has a secret ill, unseen by mortal eyes, and heal him. You could do this as you passed through the crowds. Or could you? Certainly not if you passed through the crowds as a "healer" or a wonder worker; for the moment you think yourself to be something—lo! You are nothing. And so it goes.

So you move in the consciousness of this new degree. It does not have to be held into place by affirmations or by any system that has come to you in the nineteenth century. *It is actually you.* Just as the yeast and flour are changed into bread so you have been changed into the new consciousness, and automatically you go about doing the works.

*It is thrilling to sense this,* and presently you will have much confirmation. Everything you touch, everything you say, everything you do, and all the contacts you make are charged with *Spirit,* and you have completely subordinated the idea of "might and power."

Spirit is something so natural It might be likened to the perfume of a flower. It releases itself into the surrounding atmosphere, and only by this subtle diffusion is Its presence known. As long as Spirit is something within you that has to be brought out by might or by power, it will not be natural or normal, and every time you have made a display of it, you are forced into retirement until you can again come forth with a new manifestation. Then, in the New Day, you begin to exhale the aroma (Spirit) into the world in which you live.

> Inbreathed with the breath of God, you become a living soul, and nothing but the breath of God can come from you, filled with glorious, healing light and revelation.

You may pass along the way and not meet with any so-called experiences of the Spirit within you, but *you* are Spirit, and so anyone touching the hem of your garment (consciousness) will receive the healing. More than this, new extended dimensions of the senses will come unto you. Sometimes you will know instantly that you have been brought into a situation to clarify it. It will be one of those conscious things which has its answer before the asking. And then again you will know that nothing can be done, for the failure of others to accept the Word will be too colossal, in which case you will "shake the dust from off your feet" as a testimony against them.

Sounds rather drastic, but Jesus put it this way to show you that when you are in this Father-Consciousness, the failure to bring about results for another is not to be considered or wondered at. There is no time spent wondering why it did not work. It did work, but it was not accepted, and you could do nothing more about it. In which case you shake the dust from off your feet. You dismiss it and do not go over the human facts and thoughts for a possible reason.

All this shaking the dust from off your feet is not done in the superior way of an old-fashioned practitioner trying to justify his failure. You have come to the consciousness that does not concern itself with the number or yet the importance of your works. It is just you, and the more you realize this the more you will be unconcerned about results. You will stand at the door and knock, and if any man *hear* your voice and open, you will enter in and sup with him. This partaking of substance will bring out the release that he is after and will be quite as natural as literally breaking bread with a friend.

Remember how frequently Jesus reminds you of the naturalness of manifestation? How He makes it so simple that the child can do it? Finally you begin to see.

Transformation and transfiguration take place through Spirit, which renews the mind. The renewed consciousness or new consciousness must and will bring out its own true manifestation just as the old human consciousness brings out the things it holds to be true.

In this new understanding of the Spirit, which is perforce couched in the old hackneyed language of truth, the transformation takes place first in the unseen. The temple is purged. It is changed within before the surface is touched. The changing of the unseen is so much more essential than working with the condition on the outside. The great dynamos must be perfected before the increased power can come over them to enable their outer manifestation to take on more widely diversified expressions. So, deep within you, the Spirit—which does the work—is changing the very organism of your body, replacing the old rigid "thought" ideas with the new free expression. "I shall take away the stony heart within you, and give you a heart of flesh"—the Flesh which has seen God or experienced the resurrection from the thought-graveyard.

Do you begin to sense the new and subtle revelation that is passing through us *now*? As the organs of the matter-temple become flesh, they shall see God into manifestation and shall be able to function above the level of human thought. "They shall run and not be weary" etc., etc. All this is impossible with the present worn-out equipment of the thought-world. It is glorious to sense this *Spirit* which works by Itself instead of by force (knowing the truth) or by power (trying to force God to do your bidding).

> It is all so lovely and natural, and so secret. Again the secrecy — for you are now talking about something on the new plane of consciousness, and it is all foolishness in the eyes of the mentalist. So put the coal of fire on your lips, and magnify the Lord within you.

# Chapter VII

# I Am the Resurrection

*I am the resurrection and the life ...*
*though a man were dead, yet shall he be made alive.*

And after six days Jesus taketh Peter, James, and John his brother, and bringeth them up into a high mountain apart.

And was transfigured before them: and his face did shine as the sun, and his raiment was white as the light.

And, behold, there appeared unto them Moses and Elias talking with him.

As the sense of sight is clarified and extended, it will see that which it could not formerly see. That your degree of sight cannot see "through" is no sign that it cannot be done.

This seeing through is not a psychic thing. It is not a self-hypnosis wherein one enters into a realm of shadowy beings moving about as misty forms. It is a place or elevation of sight to a degree that it sees the flesh-and-blood resurrected bodies of which Jesus spoke. "Come and see that a spirit does not inherit the kingdom of heaven." And then He showed the resurrected flesh-and-blood body, the perfectly blended body and Soul. Sight could not support the degree of vision long, and Jesus disappeared from them; yet He did not disappear any more than the radio stops broadcasting programs just because you have broken your connection.

"I am the resurrection and the life ... though a man were dead, yet shall he be made alive." I am that resurrection. Do you hear? The I AM, this Father-Consciousness in you, will eventually perform the resurrection that will be necessary if you are to overcome the last enemy, death.

The human thought shouts with derision when it hears such things, because the thickness of man's hearing makes it impossible even to imagine such a manifestation. That is why you do not go about telling people. You tell yourself and contemplate the teachings of Jesus Christ, which you profess to accept and believe. If you believe His promise that you are to do the works He did, you will have to achieve this resurrection sometime, or else you will have failed to do the things He did and cannot go on to the greater ones.

All this seems very improbable, yet the veil is so thin at this time that in the twinkling of an eye you may enter into the Light. Alone and unaided, you appropriate this new birth only when you can assume it as natural.

The vapory beings of the former imaginary heaven shall become solid and real, and you shall find they have gone nowhere except out of the dimension of your limitations. They are just beyond the limit of your double vision, and so when this vision becomes single, then you *see*.

Jesus had spent three years with His disciples, and yet when He walked with them to Emmaus, they did not recognize Him. It does not seem possible, does it? It was only possible because they believed that He had been crucified. They could not stand against the testimony of the senses which said He had died on the cross, even after He had told them again and again, "I will come again," I will resurrect this temple-body. No one believed Him. And when the women reported that they had seen Him, this was immediately denied, and an explanation had to be found for the man they had seen. "It was the gardener."

Do not then be discouraged if you have not been able to do all the works of Jesus at once. These men who were in close contact with the brightest revelator, Jesus Christ Himself, did not get it, but we have all the benefit of their actions and reactions and are beginning to *believe*, no matter what the appearances or beliefs may be.

As they walked along the way to Emmaus, their hearts burned, even as your heart burns now with the fire of Spirit. They were almost ready to take a new Master, so thrilled were they at the revelation that came to them. It is wonderful. Here am *I*—do you see Me? Or do you see the mistaken human idea and close the door on Me? Here *I* am in the midst of you. Call upon Me, and *I* will answer you.

"Arise and shine, for thy light is come, and the glory of the Lord is risen upon thee." The

81

command has gone forth, and only you can do it. No one can help you, no one can hinder you, for you have been Self-revealed; and the more natural it becomes and the more sensible and balanced it is the quicker you will go to a new mansion in My Father's house, where things are visible which were formerly invisible.

Believest thou this? In the maze of words, do not become confused and make all this lovely revelation difficult. It is simple and the child can accept it—and so can you. In fact, you are accomplishing this, else you would not be at this place of expression. You have come upon this very line to reassure you that you have already made tremendous forward steps to the attainment of this higher sight.

Ah! But presently He broke the "substance" (bread) with them, and for the space of a moment, they could sustain the extended vision and see Him; but only for a moment, for they were so clogged with excitement and sense-testimony to the contrary. But for the moment, they saw Him—no, they *beheld* Him. They were above the limitation of human sight and sound. They *beheld* Him. It was pure recognition of the accomplished thing.

*I* shall set you on fire—and the sparks shall fly upward into the night of belief and ignite it all in an intense blaze which, when the dross is consumed, will be the fire of glory. The moment you come into contact with the new revelation, everything is done by the inner fire. You are lighted up and are a burning bush, giving off the revelations with such fervent heat that it melts the hard-fast patterns of any who pass that way. You are on fire with Life and Its charm, and your fire instantly consumes all lesser beliefs in powers apart from God. You stand in the midst of your expression, a flaming, living testimony, and the word that you speak and the manifestation that you bring forth are so filled with this Light that it ignites everything in a blaze of the glory of being.

No matter what you are doing, you are aflame with power the moment you know this *Oneness*, and then the revelation pours and pours and pours out over your whole universe and fills every empty measure.

This flaming manifestation, this angel of Light which you become, sheds revelation from the next dimension to the darkened world. It is the irresistible something which draws everything unto it. "The glory of the Lord fills the house," as you, the flaming angel, let this substance pour through you into manifestation. No matter what size the measure, it is filled, "pressed down and running over." To every man—the invitation is broad and glorious—the substance of Light is pouring through the temple of this flaming angel. It is this angel who stands at the door, and the moment he is "seen," the door is swung wide open to him, and the flaming Light fills the place, and the Word which he wields is sharp and powerful and turning in all directions—

a two-edged sword. You are that flaming angel of Light standing at the door of the New Day.

This Light brings forth the transfiguration. Eventually this inner Light is going to transform the matter body to one of "flesh," one that eats and drinks and yet is not under the curse of the law of matter. The transfiguration takes place on a high mount of revelation. Do not get excited if you cannot at first rise to it, for you can never achieve this transfiguration until you can. And you only can, *when you can.* Do you hear what is now being said to you? Do you? Or do you?

This transfiguration, this sudden changing from matter to flesh, has its price. Be sure you are ready before you ask for it. "Fools rush in where angels fear to tread," and so if you were suddenly transfigured, could you take it?

"Yes, yes, of course" you could in your human thought. It thrills you to imagine you might be transfigured into the ageless, beautiful being that you actually are. But then would come the pay-off. "Discretion preserve thee." "Patience must have her perfect work," and all will be taken care of in its own glorious manner and way. The mushrooms of human thought will finally disappear, and there will be no one bearing the record of evil belief against you—the evil of age, sin, sickness, etc., etc.

Do you begin to see-hear the secrecy? It is so wonderful when you enter into the portals of this heavenly place of manifestation and see the transfiguration and see into the next degree of consciousness. You find that nothing has been lost and nothing has been changed except that matter has become flesh, and all the lovely flesh bodies were here all the time, but you could not see them because of your unbelief.

Do not become excited about all this marvelous revelation. So much lies before you that is so wonderful and grand and worthwhile that you will readily understand why the past is required by God. And you will be glad to let it go, for you are losing nothing, only allowing thought-forms to dissolve into their nothingness. Do you see?

So are you the sower of the seed. So do you stand at the portals of the New Day, the flaming angel of Light.

> "And he said, so is the kingdom of God, as if a man should cast seed into the ground; and should sleep, and rise night and day, and the seed should spring and grow up, he knoweth not how. For the earth bringeth forth fruit of herself; first the blade, then the ear, then the full corn in the ear. But when the fruit is brought forth, immediately he putteth in the sickle, because the harvest is come."

These wonderful revelations of Jesus are, when accepted, like seeds cast in secrecy and then forgotten. Day after day you go about your Father's business, and then one day the blade, and then the ear, and then the corn in the ear, and then the

85

harvest and the command, "Thrust in the sickle ... the harvest is ripe."

So will you proceed in deep secrecy to go into the New Day and be guided by the "brightness of his coming." You are the bright angel, the flaming angel with the sword, come to reap his reward. You stand, a tower of light, shedding automatically the revelation of the Presence here, there, and everywhere. It is wonderful—praise God.

Thrust in the sickle then, flaming Angel of Light. Your day is at hand. Bright messenger— Flaming Angel—you are the Christ of God.

# Chapter VIII

# Union

*There is in every union a mystic something;*
*a certain invisible bond which must not be disturbed.*
—*Amiel*

So is it. There is something so mystic in the bond between you and your Father — something so invisible and yet so wonderful that *it must not be disturbed*. It must not be broken again, this bond between you and the Father within, and it is filled with the mystic something which works entirely beyond the dimension of human thought.

It is sacred; sacred and lovely, like the refreshing sense of spring at the morn, the hillside dew-pearled, the lark on the wing, and all that Browning so beautifully writes — it is the Soul of you. Bathe deep in this lovely union, for it is mystic and shall wash away the stupid personality and its high-flown ideas of birth, race, creed, etc., or a fear of lowly origin.

"Yet a little while, and the wicked shall be no more." That is encouraging. The wicked are the scribes. Why the scribes? "Woe unto you, scribes and Pharisees!" The scribes were the historians; they recorded the lies of human findings. That is why "woe unto you, scribes!" For by the power of the inner *Union*, you are raised from the pigsty to the place of honor at the banquet table—and the former things are no more.

He who deals in the past is dead. He does not hear the command, "Let the dead bury their dead—follow thou me." He thinks he must perpetually say, "That one was a leper," long after the leprosy was nothing but a forgotten thought. Watch that you judge not from appearances, for if you believe the law, a criminal can change "in the twinkling of an eye," and while you are relating that he is a criminal, he may be that no more—in which case you are left holding the bag, which you must fill with your unbelief.

"There is in every union a mystic something; a certain invisible bond which must not be disturbed." That is the bond *you* have; that is the wonder of your New Day. You have that *mystic* union, and it must not be disturbed—and it will not be disturbed unless, through your belief in a power apart from God, you expose this lovely thing to human reasoning.

Confucius tells us something to this effect: "He who knows how will bind and use no cords, yet no one can untie; and he who knows how will shut the door, yet no one can unlock." We are not speaking of human power. We speak to you of your—*your*—God-Power, which says to the proud waves of belief, so long established by human thought-taking and history, "Thus far and no farther."

Do you begin to see what the Word is saying unto you? Do you begin to understand that you are no longer at the mercy of human belief, that you are free from words because you understand now *the Word*? John Smith has broken this Word into a thousand and one words, yet the Word remains intact, like the chain upon which are strung numberless pearls or beads. The circle of the chain is one and the pearls are many. So are the words of mankind—but the Word is one. This lovely word, *Union,* stands before you as something that is "not to be disturbed." You do not have to disturb this holy union in another, for everything you want and desire of another is yours, embodied in its own way. Believest thou this?

When you understand, even in a degree, what is this *Union* between you and your Father, you become aware of a new elevation of consciousness that daily grows more and more intimate and satisfying. You are with Him always and in all ways. No place can you go that this Father-Consciousness, by reason of its alignment with God Almighty, has not been before you. It becomes as inseparable as the yeast in the bread and permeates your entire universe. It is then a matter of simple "asking" in order to receive and "knocking'" to have secret doors opened and "seeking" to have hidden things revealed.

Do you begin to glimpse the wonder of this Father combination, or temple-Power idea? You have it with you. "I am with you always," and the moment your temple (John Smith) becomes *one* with that which has been with him always, he is stepped up out of the limitations of Jesus into the fullness of the Jesus Christ, or Father-Consciousness.

"If you go to the uttermost parts of the earth (your world), still my right hand shall lead you." It is so wonderful. You are finally conscious of what Jesus was speaking when He said, "I and my Father are one." This level of understanding immediately reveals, among other things, that the "kingdom of heaven is at hand" and that it is usable and natural, whereas before it was impracticable and imaginary.

Oneness then is possible—oneness with everything on the earth and under the earth; oneness of Life in all things. This is the influence which conquers all the enemies you ever had, for you find that the Life is *One* and that the evil interpretation under which your enemy acts is only the face value you have put upon him. He cannot act differently from the value you have placed upon him, and you think you have arrived at this value by things that he (your enemy) has said or done; whereas, in reality, your acceptance of a certain evil capacity and propensity has given him all the capacity he has for the evil manifestation. Now, with the Oneness, you can enter into the courts of this your friend, instead of the camps of this your enemy.

"Who did hinder you?" Now you understand that it would have to be yourself, for nothing can hinder you when you have made *Union* with the Father within. The belief of separated being, wandering in a world of illusion, has had its day, and you are redeemed. The moment you rise and start in the direction of your Father's house (consciousness), He, in a like moment, comes all the holy way to meet you, and the thing so precious, which must not be disturbed, is again perfect and intact. It is wonderful. "Heaven and earth are full of thee."

This union is the meeting of the prodigal and the Father. Finally the Son has returned *home* to the consciousness which has been his all the while, had he but accepted it. In that union and consciousness does he find that even though he has spent his inheritance in riotous living (this may have been in poverty, sickness, fear—all these would be riotous living), he has lost nothing, for he still has *all*. All that he spent were the shadows of human beliefs, which had grown terrible and strong as he believed in them, until he was reduced to a swineherd. We find him complaining dreadfully, feeling sorry for himself—trying to change the pigsty. But remember, a pigsty is perfect for pigs He was out of place—that was the whole trouble. Like so many other people, he was complaining about his place, yet it was perfect for its intended use—pigs.

So there is nothing the matter with the place you are in. It may not suit you, but don't waste your time trying to change it, for you will never succeed. It may be the habitat of a king and your idea of a home that of a peasant, or it may be the reverse. But if you find yourself out of harmony with it, it is because your *inner Union* is not complete, and therefore, you are constantly *out of alignment* with surrounding conditions, people, and things and will continue to blame someone for your difficulty. Once you *remember*, then you will—*because you can*—"arise and go unto the Father." Or you "will ask the Father," and remember, you have the capacity to "arise and go."

It is wonderful what takes place in your life when this remembrance comes to you. It changes everything, puts you in a state of at-one-ment with everyone and transposes things into their proper places. All things are constantly passing, and so you do not have to be possessed by them; at the same time, you do not have to destroy them just because you find them immaterial and shadowy, out of line with your individual heaven.

The only thing that is real and has substance is the Word made flesh *now*, and this coming and going out of matter and into Spirit is quite in keeping with the eternal newness of God. You see all the things about you returning to the invisible, and you are not disturbed, because they move so slowly to your sight and so normally that you hardly notice it. You think little of a flower blooming for a day and disappearing almost as quickly—yet it comes out of the invisible, holds its color and perfume to the world, and then again disappears, leaving only a memory. And you are *one* with all the trees and flowers of the universe—with everything that is about you. Everything begins to respond to the consciousness of this ineffable *Union*.

What a passport to take with you! No wonder you were told to take no thought for the purse, scrip, etc., etc., *for you have this immediate Union with the Father within, which can and does supply everything that is necessary for you.* Can you pause for a moment and flood your whole universe with the light of that single word—*behold*? You are *seeing,* for the first time, the things you are to *behold*. Your eyes are opened, and in this new light, many things that were formerly invisible are now made manifest and are found to possess qualities never before dreamed of. In this Light that comes through beholding in the *Union* of Father and Son, the ugliness of everything fades away. Age passes into oblivion, and all the writings of human thought and time on your temple are like so many pencil marks made on granite.

You have written your name—the John Smith name—all over the place and have tried to make it permanent, but the great flood of Light that comes from the *Union* of the Father and Son suddenly erases all these past acts, deeds, and thoughts, and the temple is radiant with the Presence.

Behold—Behold—Behold!

> That one word is enough to meditate upon until the Light of this Power is so consciously present that all things are made new. Behold—*I,* then, apparently make all things new, but in reality *I* only reveal that which has always been new and perfect and intact. *Even you and your temple have ever been new and perfect.*

Reduced to such simplicity that a child could and does understand it, it is now your privilege to accept this glorious Truth. *You can go now*—I feel safe for you because you have heard the *Word* of *Union*. You have suddenly become conscious of the Presence to such a degree that all things that are necessary are possible. You begin to see with the new eye and hear with the new ear, and things that you never dreamed of are suddenly in your conscious possession.

Do you begin to see? Do you know that instead of feeding five thousand people in the desert it is plainly implied that Jesus more than likely fed fifteen thousand? Tucked away in these parables are words of hidden meaning, and so we find He fed five thousand men besides the women and children! Awake thou that sleepest! You have been talking in the large number of five thousand. Suddenly it becomes fifteen thousand—and was there all the time. "Why, I never saw that before."

Well, here is a universe filled with things that you never saw before, yet they were and are there all the while—and your five thousand suddenly becomes fifteen thousand, and you cannot explain it because it has always been there in the Bible, and there is no denying that. And in this Light of the *Union* which is mystic and must not be disturbed, you will suddenly perceive how it is that "all that the Father hath is mine" and how this is the only thing that can possibly take place, for you are one with the Father—*and when you are one with a thing, you are that thing in essence* and you partake and participate in whatever its nature may be.

So, do you begin to understand why the Jesus temple-body, having nothing, yet had everything the moment it made this *mystic Union* with the Father? In Biblical words, when Jesus was able to tell the Father anything "in secret," the Father could "declare it from the housetops" because the Father is the point of contact between God and man-temple, and what He declares takes place. Thus, all things become possible to this *Union* of the Father and Son. The Trinity comes into play, and the revelation concretes itself into a something to be handled with the hands. It is wonderful.

> We are taking heaven itself out of the veils of belief and superstition and are again *one* with the whole Glory called Life, on all planes and levels. It is wonderful.

The union which has been lost sight of and disturbed is that of body and Soul. "That which God hath joined together, let no man put asunder." Your body (temple, Jesus) and your Soul (the Father-Consciousness) are discovered to be bound by an invisible bond which makes the manifestation of the power of God easy, simple, and natural; and it is this wonderful union that Jesus discovered which enabled Him to do the things that man apparently could not do. It endowed Him with the powers of the next dimension and caused Him to bridge discrepancies of human thought which could be explained only by the word *miracle*—yet there are no miracles in God; they are only manifestations which take place in a higher degree of understanding.

To the savage, the sounds issuing from the simplest gramophone would be miracle enough to warrant any sacrifice; but to you they are natural, normal, and nothing to be excited about. Why? Because you are in the consciousness which accepts the gramophone as possible, and if you care to, you can examine into and find out the infinite details of its operation.

> As soon as you arise to a new state of consciousness, all the manifestation on that plane becomes natural and normal and quite within the grasp of this consciousness. It is wonderful, for the moment you step up into the Father-Consciousness, the things that the human consciousness calls miracles are accepted as natural.

Do you begin to understand why Jesus spent no time working with appearances, knowing that it would be lost motion and accomplish nothing? But He immediately transcended the plane of evil through which He was moving, and on the next level, He discovered the nothingness of the former limitations. So His feeding of the fifteen thousand was but natural to the Father-Consciousness—and so will it be with you.

Your health will suddenly be made apparent, for you have gone up to the consciousness of Life, and the limitations of beliefs and appearances are not dealt with as something to be eliminated. In the new level, there is nothing for them to grasp, and they drop into oblivion, just as the beliefs of a savage regarding the gramophone and its supernatural powers would suddenly drop away.

"Arise and shine, for thy light is come, and the glory of God is risen upon thee." Whatever you can make your union with will come forth, for this union is the figurative male and female of God's creation and together brings forth the new manifestation. No matter what it is that you are seeking, nothing is too small, nothing too large to be brought to pass through this union.

Do you begin to understand the creative plane of Spirit? Of course, it is only the revealing of that which already is, but it seems to be created, to grow, expand, etc., to the slow consciousness of the human mind.

"Heaven and earth are full of thee." Do you understand that? Heaven and earth, your consciousness and your body, are filled with Thee—there is nothing else. And it is out of this substance of the *Thee*, which is everywhere, that the materialization takes place.

It is wonderful. What God has joined together, let no man or any kind of manifestation put asunder. There is something so mystic and wonderful in this *Union* that it must not be disturbed. Do you begin to sense this wonderful thing, this supernal *Union*?

You have come again to your heritage—your body and Soul are *one*, and the day has come

97

when it shall be proclaimed from the housetops of your kingdom, so that "he that runs may read."

# Chapter IX

# Scientific Truth

One of the great fallacies of this age is the mistaken belief that the teachings and revelations of Jesus Christ were scientific. So much has been written on this—trying to prove that science, which is purely relative and has to do with relative things, is of the same bone and structure as the power of Jesus Christ—that it has become a habit of metaphysicians to propound this idea. An apparent satisfaction seems to come to the truth student when he can make the two fit into one pattern. Yet at the very outset of his study, he finds Jesus Christ immediately departs from every basic law of science.

Always it is necessary to call to mind that the power of Jesus Christ was not of the relative world. The three-dimensional mind could not in any way grasp the idea of infinity and its capacities. The longer the argument, trying to prove that Jesus was a scientist and used scientific laws, the more confused grows the issue. Talking from two planes will bring only a divergence of results. No more will the revelations of Jesus Christ mix with the findings of man (no matter how apparently high they may be) than water will mix with oil.

The shifting, changing basis of all science and scientific discoveries has nothing in common with the immutability and changelessness of the God-law.

In recording this revelation, the intention is not to discount the marvelous things done by science on a relative plane or to in any way belittle the glorious achievements of physical scientists; it is only for the purpose of trying to clear away some of the fog that is obscuring the vision of many truth seekers.

There is nothing in science that actually will set aside the laws of gravity; yet Jesus Christ did this very thing by walking on the water. There is nothing in science which will cause the unseen to become the seen and increase five loaves of bread to five thousand. There is nothing in science which will change water into wine or produce gold in the mouth of a fish. Certainly there is nothing in science which even remotely suggests that sight be restored to those born blind and that all manner of illness and disease may be eliminated by a virtual wave of the hand.

As long as the truth student attempts to work from this basis, he is declaring one thing and knowing another, and his house (consciousness) is divided against itself and will fall.

Thousands of people who are declaring that there is no matter and that all material law is nothing are at the same instant attempting to make what is known as a financial demonstration, wherein they will handle the very matter they have just stated does not exist.

Confusing the truth of Jesus Christ with the highest findings of the three-dimensional plane, man attempts to use this law to bring about results. Jesus Christ at no time bothered with changing the appearances. He gave little or no thought to the present condition. He did not reach up or out and bring down a law and have it "work" on evil. On the plane of the Christ-Consciousness, the thing is already done. Perceiving this and keeping His attention away from appearances, He was able to see those conditions and appearances evaporate or change from inharmony to harmony.

The appearances about you might be described as congealed thought-forms. They are merely the solidification of ideas you have had in mind. The only way to destroy them is by the process of disintegration, namely, by taking thought away from them. Everything in your life is held and sustained there by conscious or unconscious thought.

The moment a thing is cut off from its supply of mental recognition, it begins to crumble.

All sorts of degrees and ideas are held over these manifestations. So we hear people say, "This is a stubborn problem," or, "Of course, this is something that takes years," or, "This is simple," etc. — and all this is relative and in the mind of the individual.

"If ye believe … ye shall say to yon mountain, be ye removed, and be ye cast into the uttermost parts of the sea, and it shall be so" does not bespeak any difficulty in handling the manifestation that seems so obdurate and impossible.

The Jesus Christ Consciousness is in operation the moment it is recognized. "It is done"—the finished mystery, the thing which is totally beyond human comprehension. And this is backed up by the instructions for true prayer: "When ye pray, believe that ye receive, and it shall be so," and "Before they call, I will answer, and while they are yet speaking, I will give it unto them."

A hundred other passages are given to show the difference in *trying to make* the law of God work and *letting* this law into manifestation through the revelation of Jesus Christ.

Not until the truth student has a clear idea of this can he have any degree of accuracy in his work. And once he does grasp the difference in the ideas, *he will go from glory to glory, from revelation to revelation*, instead of from problem to problem.

"As for man, his days are few and full of trouble." "He is a liar, and the father of it." "Conceived in sin and born in iniquity" (and a few other beautiful rules) handicap the mental creature from his very beginning. What hope has he to operate the laws of the universe unless he can ascend unto the Father before he descends unto the plane of relativity— where he can live in the world and not be of it.

This living in the world and not being of it does not mean he becomes a plaster saint, a bloodless, lifeless codfish without selection or feeling. It does

mean that he understands thoroughly the nothingness of relativity and the power of the Father-
Consciousness, to which he has ascended through
recognition, before stepping down into the realm of
manifestation. It is wonderful when you pause for a
moment and contemplate just who you are and
what your mission is.

Once you see clearly the line of demarcation
between the third and fourth dimensions, or the mental
and the spiritual, you will understand that suddenly
you have changed places. Formerly, you thought you
were here to demonstrate the power, then suddenly
you are through with "getting things," and you are
the "giver of the gift." And fear not, as the gift pours
through you into manifestation to supply your
brother's need, you shall not want for any good
thing.

> For the first time in life, you begin to glimpse
> the idea of "leave all and follow me" — and what
> a glorious invitation it is — and how you will have
> no desire to carry the little things or ideas you
> thought so precious into the kingdom of heaven.

The ascension is not through emotional imagination, nor does it deal with strange practices. It is a
pure and simple recognition of God as here, there,
and everywhere. Of course, you will at first say, "Well,
I have always believed that," but you have not, until
you can actually step into this consciousness through
the door of "leaving all" or the pure recognition that
nothing exists but God and His manifestation.

Then does the Oneness come which causes you to be one with the life in everything of the mineral, vegetable, animal, and human kingdom. If you are *one* with this life in everything animate and inanimate, you will see the control it gives you over these things.

Immediately, the human mind goes forth gladly, thinking to gain personal power. It desires nothing better than to control the universe. It comes out usually with a bad case of willpower or an astonishing ability to hypnotize itself as well as its world.

The three-dimensional mind, the mental plane, is busy always emulating the Divine. And everything that science does is merely copying the unseen law. Various methods and ways of attaining power show their apparent counterfeit basis in the final analysis, as the serpents created by the magicians resembled, to all intent and purpose, the serpent produced by the man of God—with this one difference, however: the serpent of the Lord devoured the other manifestations.

"Be not dismayed; God is not mocked" has struck a servile fear in the hearts of many who, in spite of their best teachings, still have a man-God with a group of willing workers who are spying and hunting out evil to punish. It might clear the whole situation if you said, "Be not dismayed; mathematics is not mocked." You know that if you make a mistake in mathematics, the law stands, while you flutter about in your difficulty; and this fluttering about is what you call retribution. The moment you align yourself with the principle, the mistake disappears and the place thereof. It is wonderful to feel this clean, clear flow of light filter through you.

Are you through with things and the caring of them and the seeking of them? Are you through with the attempt to sell your pigmy personality in the open mart? Are you tired of trying to keep up with the standards set for your station in life? Well, when you are tired and through with it all, then shall you have all things and do all things and be able to move your temple-body about into the place of great peace and joy, and it shall be a tower of light and refuge unto which all men will run.

It is wonderful when all the fuss and excitement is over and you come to the place of pure recognition of the Presence here, there, and everywhere—recognition of the Power which is so absolutely beyond the appearances that it could cause you to put your hand into your bosom and bring it out white with leprosy, then replace it again and bring it out clean and whole. Why leprosy? Because that was supposed to be the incurable disease, and it is given you to show how the recognition of the Father-Consciousness transcends the limited time-and-space law of the human mind.

"Look again, the fields are white." But you have just explained through your highest and most scientific findings that "it is four months until the harvest." Now, what are you going to do about it? Just which do you believe? Of course, the unascended consciousness cannot possibly understand this and is thrilled with the magic of it—thinks it would be grand if one could do it—but he has never seen it, and if he did, he would spend so much time trying to explain it away that he would miss the power of it all.

Don't you realize the necessity of ascending unto your Father? This is not a religious rite. By now you should be about ready to make this ascension because for years you have been saying that all things are possible to God and that there is nothing in the universe but God. If you can "sense" this Father-Consciousness, you will understand how it was that Jesus constantly went unto His Father, asked His Father, raised His eyes unto heaven.

*These are all states of pure recognition.* It immediately puts one in the place of perceiving the "it is done," and he is no longer concerned with the appearances, for from that moment they will start a process of disintegration, some of them vanishing "in the twinkling of an eye."

It is true that the mortal mind will be greatly inconvenienced, but what of it?

Nothing can or will stand in the way of the Presence if that thing represents evil or untoward conditions in your life.

Believest thou this? Answer me!

Do you begin to get the "feel" of the Presence? Ye shall find Me when you feel (not think) after Me. Do you begin to see the silent folding of your tent and the stealing away from it all into the midst of this blessed, pure state of "it is done"?

"Who did hinder you that you should not obey the truth?" Answer, please. A thousand and one appearances. Yet you are told to "be absent from the body and present with the Lord," to which you reply, "I have tried and tried, but nothing happens."

Nothing is going to happen because it has already happened, and when you come to the place where you are absolutely indifferent as to whether it happens or not, then will it appear because you have then accepted it.

When you have ascended to this recognition of the Presence, you will know that whatsoever you perceive in consciousness at that moment is established on the earth—without fail. Whatsoever you perceive in consciousness at this moment of ascension to the Father will come into being without fail.

How shall it come? No man knows just what the way may be. But whatever temples or bodies or situations on the mental and physical planes necessary to cause this manifestation to take place *will come into alignment,* as if they were soldiers called to attention in a well-trained army. They cannot help responding and they will not want to. The works of the Lord must be carried through into manifestation. You begin to see, then, why you are constantly told to take your attention away from appearances and keep it on God.

As you lose this false value of things and position, you gain the real importance of Life here and *now.* You gain a sense of integrity that would feed five thousand and yet pick up the pieces and find twelve baskets left. The carelessness of the human mind would cast aside the pieces because of the apparent abundance, only to find later that he was begging for a crust. There is an intense integrity in the Father-state which must be adhered to. There is lavishness but no waste, and this does not pertain alone to material things—it is also in the realm of speech and thought.

"Come out from among them, and be ye separate" is the command. Take your place, your stand, on the teachings of Jesus Christ and begin to assume the Power. "He made himself as God," and so must you. But the making of yourself as God while you are yet working on the little mental plane of things is to become an egotist.

The assumption of this power can come only when you are actually at the place of understanding why you are *no longer seeking things.* As long as you feel the desire for things and the love of them, you cannot ascend. Until they are relegated to their proper place in life, you will be possessed by them. Things are purely and simply a means to an end. They facilitate matters and make life easier and more beautiful on the physical plane, but the moment they become "valuable," they possess you and become increasingly rare and scarce. The more value you attach to them the farther and farther they recede from you.

All things are of the same value to Mind. Man places the value, and then he sets up walls over which he cannot climb. Realizing that a lump of coal and a diamond are of equal value to the Mind that created them, you can understand how the no-value and no-importance of the relative estimate of things makes it possible for you to have a sense of selectivity.

The ascension unto the Father can be made only when you realize that while you live in the midst of things and require many of them to make your heaven complete, you are nonetheless quite detached from them. This does not bespeak any disrespect or misunderstanding regarding *things*; the "pick-up-the-pieces" consciousness takes care of all this. There is full appreciation and honor given where such are required but, with it all, an unbinding of self from such manifestations as must and will disintegrate.

Do you begin to see that when you ascend to this Father, whatsoever you perceive there (whatsoever you ask in My nature) you will find in the manifest realm, without a question of a doubt? But again, if the discovery of this manifestation is going to excite you or appear as a miracle or a magic display of power, nothing will happen.

You have to go beyond the place of surprise, else you are not actually accepting it as a reality but have merely been hoodwinking yourself, hoping by assuming something of this kind to bring out the results. Nothing will happen— "God is not mocked."

Do you know for what you are praying? There is no cause for alarm, for in reality you will not bring anything very far into being that will cause any drastic reaction to you.

"My Father worketh hitherto, and I work." The *work* has already been done on the plane of spirituality, and when you ascend unto the Father and recognize and accept this without reservation or qualification— and stay on this point—then when you descend, you will "work" (do the mechanics necessary) to bring out the physical manifestation. Perhaps this will be much or little, but it will be easy and natural and filled with radiant joy and peace.

It is wonderful how we are finally making the differentiation between the mental and spiritual planes of life and how, from the Father-Consciousness, we perceive perfectly the place of the mental and the physical and do not destroy anything; we merely align the Power, thereby changing the evil condition to harmony.

"Go in and possess the land." The land (the consciousness)—go in and possess it. Stay at that ascended point, disregarding the history of your case and the appearances with their proof for or against, and possess "the land" in your soul—and verily, you shall see it into manifestation..

"Is anything hard to me?" When you are at this point of Me, you will see and understand, and you will bear away the gift. And that which you have perceived in consciousness at that moment will be made manifest on the earth-plane.

You are no longer trying to square this glorious revelation by the findings of man. It is like trying to catch light in a butterfly net. Of course, in a sense, you have caught it, but you have only circumscribed an infinitesimal bit of it. You have only made a limitation for yourself and will thereafter base all your findings of light on that which you appeared to hold for a brief moment in your butterfly net. Presently it will be gone, and you will have nothing but the stale letter of your scientific findings, and you again will be desolate and wailing, "Oh, if I could find Him."

Whatsoever you can ask the Father ..." *Whatsoever* always thrilled me as a word. It seems to be so replete with everything and so full of a sense of joy. But you cannot ask for anything in this true sense of asking (which is appropriating) unless you perceive it in consciousness, and once you do, there ceases to be a "word-asking." It is a recognition, a wordless state of recognition, a sensing and feeling of the Presence and a glorious praising of God from whom all blessings flow. Then will you see the joyous manifestation disregarding a thousand and one man-made laws of time and space.

And ye shall be fed. Do you hear? You shall
be fed. The mouth of the Lord hath proclaimed it.

111

# Chapter X

# Glorify Thou Me

*And now, Father, glorify thou me with thine own self with the glory I had with thee before the world was.*

This is the prayer that brings the answer, "Be thou glorified," for "whatsoever you ask in this nature, that I give unto thee." And this asking to be glorified with the glory that was already yours before the beginning of the John Smith (Jesus) world is merely the appropriating of the gift of God. You were created in His image and likeness and have a body which was not made by hands but which is eternal in the heavens (consciousness) and cannot fade away.

The recognition of this indestructible body, which is eternal-in-the-heavens consciousness, is the means of bringing to pass manifestations which are indeed under the caption of "miraculous" to human thought.

When Jesus Christ asked for the glory that was His before He descended into the thought-made body of Jesus, he was not asking for something that was impossible but was merely appropriating, through the *Word*, that which belonged to Him and that which would enable Him to transcend all laws of matter and belief.

"Glorify thou me with the glory I had with thee before the world was"—before you became lost in the human belief of race, creed, family, etc., etc. In the pristine beauty of Soul, you stand forth, and the "picture shown to you on the mount" is made flesh in manifestation. Eventually the transfiguration will take place, for this Light is even now fast breaking in your consciousness, and the veil is being rent asunder.

Again the word comes: whenever you *become conscious of this changeless creation of God*, you cause it to come into visibility to the degree you have accepted it as possible. If your degree of recognition is small and slow, the healing is small and slow; but if you suddenly "enter into the Father's house," then the whole thing is changed, the hopeless situation suddenly wiped out, and the picture you have conceived of the finished mystery comes to the surface of visibility.

This perfect creation, which you have been seeking through years of human expression and "through the glass, darkly" of human thinking, is moving in his sphere of perfect success and happiness. He is constantly fulfilling the divine destiny of you, and any moment you move in accord with this, your "temple not made with hands," at that instant you pick up life at the same point of success and happiness, no matter how badly you may seem to be qualified for such.

Do you begin to see the necessity of "be still, and know that I am God?" Not a man-created god who is filled with human limitations, but God the Omnipotent and Source of everything. Unto this God do you "pray-take."

"Come boldly to the throne of grace" if you expect to attain the degree of revelation which you have been seeking. It must be seen as possible now and accepted as easy and natural; and finally the assumption is made and "the glory that was yours before the world was" you now recognize *as yours*, and in a trice you are functioning therein. In a moment that you think not, you begin to experience dimensions of consciousness of whose existence you never before dreamed. If it is necessary for you literally to smite the rock and make it bring forth waters, you will do so. Or will you? You cannot do it by taking thought. *You can do it only if you can.*

A lovely serene sense of glory causes you to ascend to the new level that draws everything unto you. You are lifted to the place of substance that automatically produces money. The *love* of money has gone from you, and that being the root of all evil, you go free — into plenty. No human thought or affirmation can make this so. Thousands have tried to make money, to increase money, or to demonstrate it through affirmations; but they have failed, in spite of their elaborate courses in how it is done. Money, substance, or whatever you choose to call it, is the solidification of what you call Power. It is neither good nor bad; it is merely a convenience. It is simpler, on the gross, dense, human-thinking plane, to give a bit of matter, which in reality has no stability at all, than it is to give substance.

So in whatsoever country (consciousness) you enter, you abide there and "render unto Caesar the things that are Caesar's." In other words, if it is money you need, you must have money and not a symbolical thing called supply. And it is only when you can look this situation straight in the face that you see how you have been playing hide-and-seek with God, thinking it was more spiritual to ask for "supply" than to speak of money. It is true that sometimes it may come in another form, but it will always come in the form you can best employ to keep your kingdom of heaven—manifestation.

This perfect creation is not troubled with supply or money. It is self-sufficient. Substance, stepped down to the plane of matter, expresses the intangible substance in money or in whatever is necessary to manifest harmony. Money has no value as such.

Can you believe the invitation, "Heretofore you have asked for nothing; now ask, that your joy may be full"? Is it possible for you to *ask* now, and have it include all the former asking plus substance, in a way you have never dreamed of?

Heretofore you have asked for nothing. The little bit you wanted to pay your room rent, the mortgage, or the dress bill is nothing—that is, nothing because it is so stepped-down and so limited. *Now* ask, that your joy may be full. And suddenly the heavens open, and the blessing that descends upon you is of such a capacity you cannot receive it. It is so much more than you ever dreamed of—the Presence everywhere that suddenly becomes real and tangible—and you are given the measure pressed down, shaken together and running over, running over with substance. It is too good to be true. That is why it is true.

All the invitations of God can be accepted by you, and you alone, through this recognition. They cannot be accepted by thought, and so when you are invited to do anything, presently you will understand that you are invited because you can do that thing or because you can partake of the substance. "O taste and see that the Lord is good." Taste this precious revelation and see that you are no longer the outcast, the prodigal, struggling in a far-off country (thought) but are suddenly again in your father's house, beloved and partaking of the fatted calf.

It is through recognition of the Presence—here, there, everywhere—that you become conscious of an urge, a demand, a swift-moving desire, and following this through, you magically make the few or many moves necessary to crystallize this desire into manifestation. No man knows how—it is only that you have learned to accept the invitation.

"He shall give you the desires of your heart." Who is He, and where is He, and whose desires will

He give you? Come close to Me. You are beginning to feel this Presence and are ascending into the place of the Father within, who will give you the desires of *your* heart.

The desires of your heart are not limited and formed by any person, organization, or group of individuals. He shall give you the desires of *your* heart—that is, if you can take them. Do not grab them, do not snatch at them; just take them, accept them. The *gift* which is yours is yours; no one can take it from you. It is awaiting the acceptance only. It does not have to be created or made by you and another. It is already there, the Gift you are asking with the heart-brain. Really, you have asked for nothing, heretofore, because you have asked with the head-reasoning brain, and nothing but imagination has followed this asking.

You have asked and had not, because you were greedily looking on the loaves and fishes as substance instead of pondering the miracle that made them possible. So you finally decided that, after all, Jesus was just a man, and all he offered was words. And so it will be, again and again, until you *hear* the Word of Jesus Christ and "go thou and do likewise" because you now experience something that feel-says, "Yes, Lord—yes, Lord, I believe." And from that moment, the desires of your heart begin to come through into manifestation. It is so filled with wonder that you are carried away into the place of the most High to sit a brief moment in breathless adoration of the miracle within yourself.

"Prove me and see if I will not open windows in heaven, and pour out a blessing you shall not be able to receive." But do not *try* to prove Me—*prove* Me—go on!

It is another invitation from Spirit. It is another way of befuddling the human thought that has been trying to prove the Lord through the way of human thinking for years. It is another invitation that you can either accept or again "try" to accept.

In some strange and unexpected way, what you accept comes to pass because it is possible. The barrier of impossible is dropped when you enter the God-Consciousness of which Jesus speaks, for it is stated and established that "all things are possible to God" and in another place, "I can do all things through Jesus Christ"—but nothing through Jesus. The combination of body and Soul is so essential for the purpose of stepping down Spirit into visibility through matter, which thus becomes flesh—the Flesh that has experienced God.

Driving you on and on with the scourge of past failure is the invitation, "Go thou and do likewise," which to you becomes a command you cannot fulfill because there is nothing in the detached human consciousness that can do the works of God—it can scarcely accomplish the works of its own life. It is a difficult thing for this consciousness even to make its living by the sweat of its brow, let alone take the riches of heaven for nothing.

Yet this command, which has goaded you on and through one vale after another, finally becomes the gentlest of requests, with such a deep assurance that it is possible that you arise and go—and do … and be … and have … and take … and give.

"No good gift will he withhold from them that walk uprightly." This walking uprightly is walking with the Father, and no gift is then withheld. Then you begin to understand what righteousness is. It is perfect alignment with the Father within, in order that the works can be done through you and stepped down into visibility, given a body.

Every good and every perfect gift shall descend from the Father in heaven. The Father in another's heaven will not "descend" gifts to you. That is the mistake the thought-taking consciousness has made. It is constantly looking for a gift or help from man and is willing to ingratiate itself at the least sign of such. It will fawn on the giver as long as the gift is forthcoming and then turn and rend, the moment it is taken away. Eventually, in your on-going, there are no human gifts forthcoming, and if there are to be any more for you, they will have to come direct from the Father in heaven—the Father in your own consciousness, He who is willing and ready to give you the desires of your heart. But you will not. Why? Because you do not *believe* this, and it is impossible for you to believe because you are judging the Father by human limitations.

Yes, the gifts are to come down from the Father in heaven, in whom is "no variableness, neither shadow of turning." There is no chance of this Power not wanting to give you the gift when you approach the throne of grace with the boldness of accepting that which is offered you. There is no variableness, neither shadow of turning. Nothing is going to happen at the last minute to make Him change His Mind. It is wonderful.

"Come eat, drink, be clothed," invitations made to you and to all mankind—to the leper, the harlot, the sinner, the critic, the gossip—yea, even to that lowest of human manifestations, the malicious scandalmonger (everything shall go into the kingdom before *that* one). Yet this invitation is to such also—if it is possible to accept. It offers everything, a free and full salvation. Eat, not after the manner of another, but after the desire of *your* heart. Drink of the living waters of Life and be clothed with the garments of Light so that they may be stepped down into the garments that satisfy you on the plane of manifestation.

Can you go within and shut your door and perform all the works of the day in peace and heavenly joy? Will you be fed with Spirit and quenched with Spirit and clothed with Spirit? All these are in the realm of the unseen, but shortly they become so real to you that you do not bother to see whether or not they have materialized when you come from out the closet. But be assured, they will, once you have realized them spiritually.

So do you write your play or dig your ditch or sing your song or heal yourself or open your eyes, etc. You do all this in Spirit and it comes to pass. How? No man knows, *but it takes place*. Not to prove that God can do it, but to prove God as God. Do you begin to see or hear or sense what is written unto you this day? Revelation— revelation so filled with joy and freedom for you and for those with whom you come in contact!

Dare you accept the invitations of God? Can you do it? Can you take it? Is it too good to be true? The more you think of it, the more you decide that it just cannot happen, and it then does not happen. Dare you to enter into the Presence and perform the works set before you and contemplate this Power and magnify It and pay no attention to the manifestation? Dare you do this?

You have a desire to be embodied, and all you have to do to bring this about is to perform it in the Spirit by pure recognition that it is already finished and done, and you are but contemplating the Power which has given it to you "before you asked." You are accepting the gift in Spirit, and it will presently come into the realm of manifestation by the way of God and not by the willpower of man.

"Come unto me, all ye that labor and are heavy laden, and I will give you rest." I will give you rest from the burden of human-thinking and fear.

Invitations—"Arise and walk" to the crippled beggar of the temple. Can he do it? Can you? "Come forth" to the dead man, whose body has fallen to pieces. Was there any thought-apparatus left in a decomposed body? Did Lazarus have anything left with which to think? What is your judgment? And if he could think with a decomposed mind or brain, why didn't he get up and come out, of himself? Yet at the invitation "Lazarus come forth," he arose and came forth, for "I have power to pick it up and lay it down" (life)—and so have you, and so, manifestly, had Jesus.

We are beginning to sense the power of Jesus Christ, and it is just this recognition that is enabling us to come forth and *let* the Light of revelation shine from us. *I* will speak through you and walk through you; and work and play and sing and dance through you. All these wonderful things will *I* do through you. *Make way for Spirit, and all human thinking must give way for Spirit to come into manifestation.*

"Acquaint now thyself with him, and be at peace: thereby all good shall come unto thee."

> Acquaint now thyself with this Father within and be at peace, and you shall see perfection of Life manifested everywhere. Yea, you shall be glorified with the same glory you had with God before the world was. Selah!

# Chapter XI

# The Past

*God requires the past.*

This might be said in a half-dozen more popular ways. For instance, if you throw a log of wood on a fire, the entire "past" of the wood as acorn, tree, and wood must go, in order that the new manifestation of heat and light may take place. While this illustration is entirely unsuitable to an act of God, yet will it cause you to understand that if the new consciousness is to take place in you, *the past* must be consumed. There is nothing to salvage, for there is nothing in it but a record of heart-breaking failures or temporary successes, of losses and unhappiness or joys that have become memories which may bless but more often burn.

God requires the past. Do you want to release it, or do you want to "save your darling from the flames" and have the new manifestation also? This question should be answered before you ask for the new consciousness. Of course, in reality, you can get nothing while you hold onto the old idea, and so you "ask and receive not, for ye ask amiss, that ye may consume it upon your lusts"—the lust of personal recognition; the asking for spiritual power in order to shine as a great personality with great spiritual understanding. The lust after spiritual recognition shows that the old consciousness with its past has not been given over to God.

It is not strange that at this stage of things there is a sudden pause, for straight is the way and narrow is the road that leadeth unto salvation. This straightness is not in the old sense of the word but is a natural shortcut. You have found out in mathematics that a straight line is the shortest distance between two points. And it is narrow, for it admits of absolutely nothing but God. This narrowness is Infinity, a strange but paradoxically true statement. So narrow is it that no personal opinions or beliefs, no systems, no persons, places, or things have anything to do with it.

So wide is the road that leads to destruction that it covers the entire mental thought-taking field. It is filled with uncertainty and is constantly asking the question, "Is this he that should come, or look we for another?" If you still have to ask this question, it is because you are looking for a man or a system of ideas to get you into heaven, and you are on the broad highway which is filled with dissenting voices. Each group is talkily building a Tower of Babel (babble), every man, woman, and child being sure that his is the only way to enter heaven; and in this very effort to build a tower to heaven, he shows he has failed to grasp the truth that he is already in heaven and is going nowhere but into a new state of consciousness. He is entering into the "flesh" which has experienced the change expressed by "yet in my flesh shall I see God" and which is conscious of dimensions it formerly knew not.

The broad highway wherein every sect is building a tower to heaven is filled with confusion. Each workman on the tower begins to develop his own idea and puts his own words into the mouth of the leader, until the whole thing becomes such a jumble that it collapses. The self-opinionated workmen run from the falling towers and immediately begin to explain all the deficiencies of their materials. Those who have been loudest in praise are now strongest in condemnation.

Then the old human thinking is off on another chase. A new Messiah has come in another person; fabulous stories of "demonstrations" are circulated, and these are greedily eaten up by the seeker. He immediately magnifies them beyond all reason and starts to build a new tower to heaven. Every last living builder is working for one sole purpose: to be first into the kingdom of heaven and to get a pat on the head for his noble work. That is one reason why all such, building towers to heaven, would fail anyway. They are out for personal aggrandizement or for getting something to satisfy their greedy human selves.

Anyone still looking for a new Messiah is still on the broad highway, still building towers to heaven instead of being in the narrow way of Infinity. Instead of recognizing that the kingdom of heaven is within, he clings to the belief that he must make a temple to it. A temple "made with hands," which must pass away. His best judgment of the success of his work is how many people can he draw into his temple or how large and impressive the place from the outside.

All such temples made by hands will pass away, and the builder will be defeated, hurt, and turned awry until he grasps this simple teaching of Jesus and throws into the flames of Spirit the entire bundle of junk he has taken on.

The temple that man is to discover, or have revealed to him, is the one "not made with hands and eternal in the heavens (consciousness)."

> The temple that already is heaven here and now is that which has eternally been; and all this symbology unravels into the simple law of accepting, unequivocally and without reservation, the revelation of the Master, Jesus Christ.

So filled with joy of this discovery is man that he is ready to "give the past" to God. In other words, he draws a watertight door between himself and that which has gone before. He exchanges the limited personal sense of Life for the impersonal, and this immediately repersonalizes itself, free from the past or the history of the evil against which he has put up such a losing fight all these years. "If you lose your life, you shall find it." If you lose this pygmy personal life in the Infinite, then shall you find your real Life, which offers the temple not made with hands, in which to dwell and in which to make manifest the new light of revelation.

If you suddenly experience what it is to lose this little personal, struggling sense of things for the great impersonal Life, you will know you have given up nothing when you allow God to "require the past." It is like giving up the cocoon when you have finished with it and have no longer any use for something which records the history of your past existence as a grub.

Do you see that what is required of you is only something with which you are entirely through? You are not asked to give up a single thing worth anything to you. You are simply awakened to the fact that you have been hanging on to empty shells (which you have outgrown) and at the same time trying to be rid of the bondage they imposed upon you. This is surely the house divided against itself and doomed to fall.

The same idea is expressed in "cast your burdens on Me, and I will sustain you." The moment you cast the past onto the shoulders of Me, it is disintegrated and presently is no more. Do you see the difference between the new consciousness, which comes into being when you have allowed God to "require the past," and the old idea that you still had some "work" to do on the hulk of your past?

Up to the very moment you discover this,
you work with past conditions that are with you

only because you keep feeding them with the one thing they can live on—your thought.

Thought is the life of all evil. It sustains and keeps it going, and the whole of your past, which is really so unimportant to another, is only kept in place by your thought. Memory of an accident, and not the accident itself, is responsible for the effects of that accident today, no matter how much your human mind may fight against this.

Of course, this is only true in the Jesus Christ revelation wherein you are "born again" and "must be born again." Breaking the thought-stream to the past will cause the past to disintegrate. Already it is nothing but a memory to you. So much of it is important only to you, and if you could not remember it, it would lose *that* importance.

> The moment it is dropped from your consciousness, it is dropped from the only place it ever existed.

You think you have thousands of testimonies against you, but the moment you have dropped the past in consciousness, it is gone. "Where are thine accusers?" There are none as soon as the idea is dropped from the consciousness of the one accused. This does not bespeak license, but liberty, freedom from the bondage of the past which you have bound to yourself like a terrible weight of oppression. As long as you thought it was real, it seemed to be there—but suddenly it is dropped from you, and then it is gone forever.

The human mind imagines the past is much more important to others than it really is, and in some strange way, imagines that all other people have to do is to remember the evils it has done. Examine a little into this. Your vanity will get a shock when you find that you are not that important. As a human being, you are going to pass away; you can last only so long, that is, if you do not bring about the union of body and Soul. You cannot by "knowing the truth" hold this old structure into place. It is a record of the past, a history of all the evil, an account of all the fear, age, limitations, disease, etc., etc., that you have had during your lifetime in this body, unenlightened and uninspired.

How marvelous it is, this requiring the past, when you *see* it. When you suddenly understand that you are the only one holding the past into place, what a sudden cleansing and freedom comes when you "loose it and let it go" and enter into the New Day. You will lose nothing that is real and will be able, for the first time, to go free into the New Day, for the shackles which have bound you all these years have been the hindrance that has kept you from your heaven-on-earth.

"Awake thou that sleepest, and Christ shall give thee light"—awake and arise from the dead! Do you hear? Yes, the light is breaking over you as you read; and as I write, I am standing in lovely agreement with you.

I am speaking this to *you*, even though I do not know you in the flesh. I am now sending it along to you, and one day you will come to this recording of the Word, and everything will burst into light—a light so bright as to make midnight as noonday.

You will see for the first time what the Scriptures say unto the churches (temple bodies), and you will pause a moment and praise God from whom *all* blessings flow.

Do you begin to experience the automatic power which is even at this moment operating in you? We have automatically, you and I, made to descend divine blessings—the All-Blessings—and everything is being flooded with them. And the littered, futile past is being loosened from its old mooring and is about to float away into oblivion, and naught is left but blessings which you automatically share with everything you consciously touch.

You are breaking bread at this instant with everything, for "the former things are passed away; they shall not be remembered or come into mind anymore."

It is so wonderful—all the old heavy stumps of hatred, resentment, injustice, and the like are gone forever. Even the memory of them is passed, and you are standing in the light—yourself the Being of Light. Do you hear-see? Do you sense the whole lovely automatic unity that is possible when "two shall agree" as we are agreeing at this moment?

*I am recording this for you.* I AM is speaking unto you, for the Voice is not mine (the recorder's) but His who hath sent me into expression. It is the Voice which is even at this moment precipitating the flood of blessings on you. Suddenly you are out in it—the life-giving rain and downpour of substance. It is permeating every cell of your body, your Consciousness, your house, your world. "Heaven and earth are filled with thee." The glory of the Lord is filling the house and is shining forth from your temple with such a power of illumination that everything that touches you at this high moment will be healed —healed without knowing the flesh source from which it comes.

From now on, you will begin the automatic process of revelation. At the mere mention of the Word of Jesus Christ, a glorious vista of new joy will be yours. This is spoken to you from Spirit, from the Father within me to the Father within you, and it is so. There is Life everlasting in the Word, and it is this touch of Life everlasting which shall release Itself to you, now that you have seen what is the Word of Jesus Christ. It will come into being with such bliss and joy and such freshness and freedom that you will never again think of words, but the Word of Jesus Christ, and you will never again hear the Word without experiencing a great burst of thanksgiving.

You live "not by bread alone, but by every word that proceedeth out of the mouth of God." You drink of the Word, and you breakfast with the Word, and you are suddenly "about your Father's business" because you have given up the tedious business which had to do with the worn-out past you had been carrying along with you, lo these many years.

God requires the past. Can you give it to Him? Are you ready to leave the husks which you have outgrown and which are tiresome to others who have had to put up with them because human fate so decreed? Are you ready to discard the whole thing and "come unto Me"? The first time you wanted to come, you thought too much about it, and on the think-plane of things you cannot walk on the water, so you floundered and sank. But you are at the point of again asking Me, and *I* am at the point of again saying, "Come," and this time you will make it to the boat of realization. For you are not again going to descend to the past, with its laws of fear and evil, but will keep your mind stayed on Me, and this time you will reach the boat.

Keeping your mind stayed on Me is not such a task when you have let God require the past, for there is not a lot of unfinished business—hate, envy, getting even, etc.—to take care of. You have nothing to go back to, for the former things have already passed away, and they shall not be remembered nor come into mind anymore.

Yes, I know that the boat of manifestation, or materialization, will be reached many times, now that your mind is stayed on Me. Whenever you ask, I say, "Come," and if you can see the light in this, you will always reach the boat without help. You will reach the manifestation over and over again and with increasing ease and joy. You will discover a new sense of well-being stealing over you, a new feeling of freedom and peace, for the great weight of the past is no more, and you are free.

> "I shall remember your iniquities no more." "Though your sins be as scarlet, they shall be white as snow." The past with its hate, criticism, poverty, envy, and disease shall be no more. God has required and received the past.

# Chapter XII

# Contact (Touch)

*Pure truth cannot be assimilated by the crowd;*
*it must be communicated by contagion.*

*—Amiel*

"Who touched me, for I perceive that virtue has gone out of me?"

Do you suppose the physical touch of Jesus was any more efficacious to heal disease than your physical touch? The contact of Jesus' touch was made in consciousness, and *whenever this contact-touch is made, something happens.*

In a radio studio, the word *contact* means much. It completes the final hook-up, and the program, which has been inaudible until that moment and which is now audible only in a comparatively small room, can be sent over the entire world. Without the contact, it would be communicated only to a few people within physical hearing distance; but with contact, it goes over thousands of miles and reaches millions of people, who hear with the same ease as those in the small room. The magic of this illustration shows what is, in the physical sense, touch, when it is extended into the consciousness of the Father within. It releases whatsoever it will into the universal, and it reaches anything that is attuned to it.

So the woman of the Scriptures (the John Smith) making contact, or touching the Father-Consciousness, is sure to receive the "virtue" of this contact and be healed or transformed or changed in some way.

So is it with you. When you touch, or contact, this Father within, you immediately bring about a new manifestation, and you know within that "virtue has gone out" of you. You are conscious that something has taken place, and you can now give thanks that the releasement of that which you touched, or contacted, in the unseen is about to take on a body and a form. You remain serene and free from the anxiety of doing anything.

When a radio announcer is to speak a great distance, he takes particular care not to increase the tone of his voice, yet the human mind would urge just such a course. It would shout, hoping thereby to increase the power of the word. But it would defeat its own purpose, and the diaphragm of the microphone would vibrate so that the words would be lost.

So with you. When you "touch," you do not increase the quality of it or the intensity of it, else you disturb the effects by your unbelief. For in the understanding of the Word, we find that intensity of expression or repetition or anxiety for results all indicate a lack of understanding. Witness the uninitiated, who thinks that by shouting he is increasing the potency of the spoken Word.

When Jesus said, "I will; be whole," He did not shout it, and when He reached out his hand and raised the dead, He did not use force. Any attempt to do this would have shown a physical sense of limitation at work, and the results would have been nil. It is wonderful when you begin to perceive the sense of touch as explained by Jesus Christ and as shown forth in a thousand illustrations.

When you touch anything, you transform it if you touch it with the Consciousness of the Father within. "Give him a cup of cold water in my name (*nature*) and forbid him not." Do you see the potentialities in the power of contact, touch? Therein lies the ability to transform substance literally as well as figuratively, so that a glass of cold water becomes the elixir of life to the one to whom it is given. Do you believe this? Do not try to prove it for the simple sake of seeing whether it is so or not, for then it will not be so. Rest all this idle curiosity in "the place of the dead." Let it sleep with its fathers and forget all prying human thought the while you are in the way of contact with the Power.

So you see that you then have this divine touch, and everything with which you come in contact is changed. The desert shall blossom as a rose — literally and figuratively. Any desert state of consciousness shall blossom as a rose when you contact or touch this Presence.

*Make it increasingly simple and natural* — divorce the whole thing from the preconceived notions that it is something special and supernatural or that you are performing a difficult task.

> You are touching the hem of the robe — the Oneness — and you are healed, launched forth into the flood of manifestation. It is natural, it is normal, and it is a power which is yours by reason of your divine heritage.

"Arise and shine, for thy light is come, and the glory of God is risen upon thee."

Arise — do you hear? Arise from chaotic beliefs and limitations. That is what you are about to do when making the contact; the touch will come through by the "way ye know not of."

"He laid his hands upon them and healed them." He made the contact; he "touched" them. Do you begin to grasp the God-given power that lies within you and why you are sent unto all the world? With this touch of contact alone, you can be unafraid to go forth into expression, for whatsoever you touch with this consciousness breaks into bloom. Do you see?

Now "two shall agree as touching" on any point, and it shall be established on the earth. As touching — as contacting — do you see how the sense of touch is extended into the agreement, or the fulfillment of the thing agreed upon? If you can touch-contact the Father-Consciousness, your agreement is bound to take on form and shape and shall

137

be established on the earth. That is, it shall take on a physical body and form—shall come into visibility by the "touch" or contact.

As the revelation of the Jesus Christ teaching comes to you as an actuality, you will know that each of the five senses must be released into its full capacity. We have had proven to us that not one of the five senses is reliable. Jesus openly addressed a group of so-called normal people as having eyes and seeing not, and ears and hearing not, plainly inferring that something lay beyond the limit of the present consciousness of the human senses.

Is that what He meant? That state where each of the senses is extended into a new field of expression and takes in an infinitely wider scope than it now has? When the senses become spiritualized, all of the functions suddenly extend into unknown fields of activity.

As the sense of touch is released from the narrow confines of being merely that which comes into contact with some single object, it goes out and "makes the agreement" by touching the Oneness of everything. It rests upon a so-called condition and, with the touch of a feather, breaks through an iron gate of resistance. All this is unexplainable to the human consciousness of the five senses, but it has its place in the New Day. So you are beginning to realize what the dimensions of the human senses can be, when understood.

.

As Jesus and the centurion understood the law of authority, so also did the centurion realize how the consciousness of Jesus Christ could reach out and touch the stricken servant across intervening miles and call upon the Father within that servant's consciousness to come forth—with the result that "the servant was healed in the self-same hour." It all seems vague when put on paper, but between the lines of this message is the Spirit which will enable you to release the senses one by one and give you the power to perceive the next dimension.

When you feel a thing in your heart, when you conceive of it as a reality, then you can make this *touch* which releases the "virtue," or completion, of the agreement. "If I could but touch the hem of his robe, I should be healed."

Plenty of people had all day long crowded about Jesus with no special results whatsoever. They had touched Him physically without healing—yet one *touches* Him and virtue goes out. So you, as a so-called healer, know when virtue has gone out; your touch has been accepted by the one who feels it as a reality and has thus made the circuit of reality to become manifested in the flesh.

Do you claim that sense of touch which enables *you* to feel-touch in making the agreement and to see it established in the world? Then it is so, and so it is.

Transmutation is within the power of touch, the real, conscious touch—the consciousness that reaches out and touches the blind eyes through the laying on of hands, or even without the physical hands, and thus transmutes disease to terms of life. The power expressed in all evil is gathered up, as a live wire would be if fallen to the ground. The minute power is taken away from any manifestation of evil, it ceases to exist, for such is fed and sustained only by thought. Everything with which you *now* come in contact is permeated with Spirit because you have touched it. "Who did touch me, for I perceive that virtue has gone out of me." I perceive that the agreement has been touched, and the manifestation is about to come forth.

More and more, as you accept the revelation of Jesus Christ—the Spirit made flesh and the flesh made Spirit—do you see the necessity of pure assumption. There is no way of acquiring this new dimension through thought, for you are told that the corruptible body is the body of limitation; that which left Paradise and wandered far afield; that which, having eaten of the forbidden fruit of the Garden, knows evil and consorts with it through imagination, hypnotism, and a belief in two powers. Its eye (consciousness) is double and takes into its consciousness every passing scene. It is immune from nothing and can make no sure and steadfast statement of itself, for it is "a liar and the father of it."

No wonder Jesus did not stand aghast at the million and one evils that were presented to Him as real and true, when He knew the worst case of leprosy to be as unreal as the slightest cough. At no time did He sympathize with the victim of the so-called disease but stood blandly indifferent to the greatest appearance of evil—in other words, death. It was this divine indifference which enabled Him to walk right through one thought-picture after another. At no time was He moved by the picture, but often He was surprised that His disciples and followers continued to see affliction as real and failed always to see the Power instead of the manifestation.

Jesus touched His Father-Consciousness, and then the two became One, and the deck was cleared for action. For at that moment the entire power of the universe was ready and willing to pour through into manifestation at His behest. It is wonderful when you understand this Trinity in Unity (Oneness) and how every man has it within him and, by this very having it within him, becomes one with the universal whole. Surely, then, it can be understood how "the lion will lie down with the lamb."

But assumption is necessary because it is above the think-process and automatically appropriates that in which it believes. Man will finally arrive at the point where he will recognize his own Godhead. He has trusted in himself (the human ego) so long and failed so often that it seems difficult to cast all his burdens on *Him*. But as his mind is purified of the desire to make himself great or to be known of his works, will he begin the lovely process called assumption.

He will appropriate and magnify the Lord within him and without, until he can "go in and possess the land" and can "decree and it shall come to pass," and finally prayer will become a natural, normal process. The praying without ceasing will go on in the constant joy of daily living, and the special pointing of it in the case of a so-called problem will be through fasting—a sudden cutting-off from every last human belief and a staying with the Father within, until the confidence is again so established that when man "looks again," the answer is with him in the flesh.

It is wonderful to contemplate this touching the Father, and this touching is the agreement. Do not think in degrees of hardness or easiness in God. It is all natural and normal. There are no big problems in the God-realm. The bigness or littleness exists only in the consciousness of you, and what is a terrific problem to you is nothing to another.

> Do not be deceived by the appearance, but at the same time, do not think because you shut your eyes to appearances that you have met any issue. Stand and look at it—but look through, taking your attention away from it, keeping your consciousness on your Father, who can bring to pass whatsoever you desire.

When Peter was cast into prison, he stood with this serene indifference. He was never once in prison as far as he was concerned—thence, the impossibility of human thought keeping him there.

If it took an earthquake, what of it? What matter how the mortal thought or pattern is disturbed? What matter if it is blown to bits—if mortal thought still insists on the reality of the condition which you have dropped off, it will have to stand the consequences (earthquake) together with its destruction of every last shred of the consciousness which insisted it was true and real. But what happens to it is of no importance. You are not concerned, so be not dismayed. "My ways are not your ways," saith the Lord, "for my ways are as high above your ways as the heavens are above the earth."

Do you see what divine law says? My ways are as different and high above your ways as the heavens are above the earth. Ponder this in your heart, and you will begin to understand why Jesus knew what He could bring to pass when He touched the Father within. He knew that the Power which was to operate was so much above anything the human mind had conceived that there was no need to wonder whether it could perform or not.

So the touching, in the spiritual sense, is as high above mere human touching as the heavens are above the earth—*for when you touch Me, you set in motion the power of the invisible, and something takes place.* Something must take place. The glory of the Lord fills the house (consciousness) of the one touching, and to the relative world, he is healed or prospered or changed. The only place such things can take place is in the temple-body, or relative world of manifestation, for nothing has to take place in the Father-Consciousness, or heaven. It has already happened there.

It is wonderful how the Truth is flooding in upon us and how you will presently make the assumption of the *Word* of Jesus Christ, disregarding every word of mankind, and will go forth and "lay on the hands," literally or figuratively, and perceive virtue going out from you. You will be able to "give to any man that which he asketh," and it will be just what he actually needs to complete the circle of his problem.

Nothing of the next dimension is going to happen to satisfy your curiosity. If you are still curious, it is because you do not believe. You only want to, and you think you are doing a noble thing when you say, "Well, if I could only see, I would believe." The blessing goes to that one who does not need a sign, for the signs will follow—they will not precede. It is wonderful.

When it becomes so natural and normal with you that it is not a surprise or a matter of concern over the results, they will be forthcoming one hundred percent. You will then go your way, having spoken the Word, and all will be well.

Suppose others do not accept the agreement you have made with them. That does not damage your consciousness. For when you have made your assumption, every word that you utter in the light of this revelation shall come to pass. You are a prophet (see-er). You will be able to do away with any thought concerning the how and why of anything. You will become so conscious that your body is the temple of the living God that the light will shine through it and many will see it. And some may touch it in the press of life and be healed.

You will finally *sense* that what you are saying is being materialized in the one to whom you are speaking. It will be the *click* of the agreement, consciously made on your part but unconsciously accepted on the part of the other. Then may he exclaim to you, "My God and my Lord," in some form or other. He does not have to say those words, but what he does say will be in the line of recognition of the "virtue" that has gone out of you. At last you are finding out why you came unto this world.

Do you now understand why and how you are to go into all the world and preach the gospel, heal the sick, raise the dead?

In the ancient fable of "Midas and the Golden Touch," we glimpse something of the possibilities of you when you are awakened, without the hampering human limitations. Whatever you touch mentally or physically or spiritually feels the impact of this subtle touch and is changed.

*Who touched Me?* And then, one of these moments, you will ask, "Who touched me?" (the little John Smith), for you will perceive that virtue has gone out of the one and has entered into you.

You, too, may have the golden touch, the touch that releases, that fulfills, and this sense of touch is finally expanded into its supreme capacities.

# Chapter XIII

# Hear Ye

*The voice of one crying in the wilderness,*
*Prepare ye the way of the Lord.*

The Voice at the door, waiting to be heard. The Voice of Jesus Christ as audible, or more so today than it was two thousand years ago.

The Voice.
*I* am the Voice.
*I* am *the* Voice.
*I am the Voice.*

Speak the word (can you hear it?), and the servant shall be made alive. "All right, I will"—and the servant, a long way off, heard and was healed.

Hear ye! Hear ye! Make way for the Lord!

Moses putting his hand in his bosom and taking it out white with leprosy and then repeating the action, once more showing it fair of flesh—this is power in manifestation. Moses is simply going from the human thought to the Divine and back again, or vice versa. He is manifesting what Moses, as an unenlightened man, could easily have had—leprosy —and then is showing the complete dominion over human belief by going unto the Father-Consciousness within.

This is given as an illustration of what eventually must and will come to pass in you. You will be able to open the door and let Me in to sup with you when you *hear* My voice—but not before. Until that hearing takes place, you will be hearing a John Smith voice, and it will be filled with the limitations of John Smith. You will not be able to open the door to your Lord but will be able to peek through the keyhole of the door of John Smith and see a certain light. But "I stand at the door (of your consciousness) and knock, and if any man (I do not care who) hears my voice and opens unto me, I will come in to him and sup with him and he with me."

"Having ears ye hear not." You are fully equipped with ears, but you cannot hear. It is rather insulting to human intelligence to be told that it is hearing nothing of what is being said, that it hears imperfectly through its own limitations, and that what it hears only vaguely resembles the Word that has been spoken. "Having ears, ye hear not."

"Then shall the ears of the deaf be unstopped," and they shall hear; and when they hear in the new hearing, they shall be able to hear the command of the Master, "Go into all the world, preach the gospel." Open the eyes of the blind; open the ears of the deaf; raise the dead, etc., etc. All these things shall they hear understandingly instead of with the testimony of the unhearing ear, charging them off to the impossible.

Through the recognition of the Presence, you shall be able to extend the sense of hearing beyond the narrow confines of the physical ear. You shall be able to hear the spirit of the Word instead of the letter, and out of the tomb—the dead letter tomb—will come the resurrected thing, and with it all power to bring itself into manifestation.

"The dead shall hear my voice and shall live." The voice of this Father within shall go into all your world and call to life all the wonderful ideas and beautiful desires and early dreams which have been dead, lo these many years, and they shall arise into manifestation. This new calling will make real all the symbolical phenomena which you have known and cherished so long. Yes, the dead shall *hear* for the first time because the hearing has been suddenly awakened (extended) to the dimension of Spirit.

He who hears obeys, and the obeying is not in the nature of being forced to do something because of a command, but a loving willingness to do because it is now easily possible of beautiful accomplishment and no longer a heart-wearing attempt to make something impossible take place.

You will "go" when you *hear* the Voice, when you begin to see that you are never commanded to do anything that you cannot do perfectly, easily, and naturally. When Jesus said, "Go into all the world," it was because He knew that anyone hearing this could do just that and could accomplish all the things commanded of him. From that moment of hearing, he no longer tries to perform the works but goes and does likewise because he has *heard* that it is all natural and possible. His temple goes forth and is ready to perform the mechanics, finding within itself all the substance formerly lacking.

If you hear the Word, "take no thought of the purse, the scrip, the ring, the robe," etc., but "go." If you hear this "go," you will find that all the props in the new play of Life will take care of themselves and that no limited human thought or deaf-hearing consciousness can, or may, enter into the out-rolling of these beautiful manifestations. You hear My voice and you "do" —because you now "hear-do." To hear is to *do* from this level of consciousness, but from the human thinking it is to *try* to do.

If you cannot *hear*, you will not recognize Me when you see Me; you will not know Me when I meet you at the crossroads, laden with props which belong to your new play of Life, for you will be dull of ear and fearful lest the very thing that is here to help has come to hurt.

The memory becomes perfect when you appropriate the clarified hearing, because "I shall recall to you whatsoever I have said unto you" is true, if you have *heard* it. If you have only heard words, then you cannot recall it.

The hearing ear, the new dimension of hearing that is yours for the acceptance, enables you to hear the Voice and to obey it, for this sense of hearing is replete with an assurance that manifestation can and will be brought forth—it is already done. How and why and when it will take place on the physical plane is of no importance. Suffice it to say it will come into visible being because it has already been done in the invisible.

This is the voice from behind: "turn to the right … turn to the left." Do you hear? Do you begin to understand a little of what we have been missing because we have had ears and no hearing—only a tinkling of sounds which meant nothing?

As "the power of life and death is in the tongue" so is the power to accomplish in the hearing; so in the hearing of the Word is the possibility to bring forth into manifestation, for "My words are spirit, and they are truth," and they "shall not return to me void, but shall accomplish whereunto they are sent"—if anybody can hear them and permit them to come into being. But the deaf ear hears nothing, and the so-called hearing ear hears only its own interpretation of power.

There is an awakening to this hearing of the Voice of God, the Voice of God speaking to you, which you have refused to hear, lo these many years. You are afraid to assume the truth of your being because all the senses have been so stopped down that they could not believe. But now you are arising into the recognition of the Presence and going freely and naturally to the Father and hearing the Word of Life.

My Word then becomes your word, and the Voice of God is heard again in the land, speaking through the temple of you; and the cleansing of that temple goes on, almost furiously to the human sense of things—so many beliefs pass away, and so many lies dissolve into nothingness, and the vacuum left by human beliefs is filled to the brim with the Presence.

Think of it. When you *hear*, you can go into all the world and accomplish what Jesus has told you was possible of accomplishment. You have a constant stream of guidance from within you, for behind the whole thing, the Father-Consciousness is now directing the son in his goings and comings; and presently he will find that he has entered into the door of the sheepfold and that he may go in and come out and find pasture. Surely he will presently say with joy, "The lines have fallen to me in pleasant places." I shall go in and come out in peace.

That is the freedom of Spirit of which Jesus spoke, in contradistinction to the efforts to break away from human bondage. You have tried so hard to hear, and you have wanted so long to see; both of these gifts are yours, but they must be taken as gifts, else you will never manifest them.

Do you believe? Do you accept? *Then you will stop trying to hear and you will hear*, and so with seeing. You will not try to "prove Me" for any reason whatsoever, but you will prove Me because that is the natural action of the law, moving from the invisible through your consciousness and solidifying or becoming flesh. The Word that you hear shall not return unto you void but shall accomplish whereunto it is sent, and when you listen now for the Voice, you will hear because you have accepted it as the Father's Voice in the midst of you.

The so-called clairaudience, so much talked of as a special gift of the occult, is not only possible, it actually exists in your God-Consciousness. And if you have heard "whatsoever you ask," you might as well ask for this clear-hearing, because it is time that you heard every word, human or divine, that has to do with you. It is part of the equipment of the new man. Why should you go about in ignorance when you have capacity to *hear* anything that has to do with you? Do you believe it? Well, then, you will see-hear it into manifestation. *You cannot miss a thing.*

That is why, when you hear the Voice of the Father within you as *you* and are thereby connected with the Universal, no secret can be kept from you which has to do with your on-going. Nothing can be kept from you. There is no key or secret lesson that any man possesses of which you cannot instantly avail yourself. *There is no secret or key lesson in God. There is no great discovery which is not your discovery.* And it cannot be sold to you. It is yours now. Do you hear?

Glory to God that you are *hearing* for the first time the promises of the Bible, and they are kept and fulfilled—every last one of them.

You can begin to understand now why Jesus said, "The works that I do, ye shall do also, and even greater works than these shall ye do." Now you can hear-believe, hear-accept, hear-recognize, hear-appropriate—for hearing is so closely allied with doing that the cripple, who for forty years had heard nothing but evil and was steeped in limitations, etc., suddenly "hear-leaped" into the New Day.

That is the way of Spirit. When you *hear* anything from your Father, it jumps into action. It is the thing which acts and impels you to change your environment so that the static becomes the active and you are resurrected from the dead beliefs that have held you so long.

When you *hear* the Father within you say, "I see thee whole," that means that you "hear-leap" into wholeness. You first tell your Father something in secret, and the Father, hearing in secret, calls it from the housetops, and the manifestation leaps into joy. The Father within cannot hear you, and you cannot tell Him anything in secret, unless your hearing is clarified to a point that it can hear the answer. So long have you told the Father things in secret, and nothing has happened—because you could not hear Him when it was being "called from the housetops."

Strange, is it not, that all this time we have thought the Father within or God outside didn't want us to have the manifestation. And now we see that He gave it to us every time and called it from the housetops, but we could not hear it and thought our praying was in vain, and sorrow filled our hearts.

Yes, ye shall tell the Father—your Father—and this being the point of contact between you and God, your desire is called into manifestation. When you call from this Fatherhood degree, it is as if a huge magnet were introduced into a plane whereon were millions of particles of steel; they rush automatically to the magnet. So will the atoms draw themselves into the pattern of the Word. On the matrix of your prayer will this substance suddenly take shape and reveal itself as that for which you have asked. But only if you can hear; otherwise you do not know what are the mechanics that must be performed to accomplish the outpicturing.

Presently you see that the use of many affirmations is accomplishing nothing, that it is the practice of the heathen and posits a consciousness which believes that God does not hear except much repetition be used—and then only rarely answers. To what kind of a God pray ye? To the One which Jesus came to show forth when He said, "Before you ask, it is answered, and while you are yet speaking, it is given unto you"? Do you want that kind of a God? Or one to whom you have to plead and make sacrifices in order to have that which is necessary for everyday life?

For your Father knoweth your needs before you ask. He does not have to hear sounds. It is actually strange that we should have to make so many sounds with the lips in order to convey a state of consciousness. And it is true that when two are perfectly attuned, they talk less and less yet know more and more of each other. They begin to hear without the use of words, for they sense the *Word*.

The Word is heard, and it goes into the heart of man. It is wonderful. "There are many things I could not tell you in Jerusalem because of your unbelief."

# Chapter XIV

# The Sense of Smell

The sense of smell has, through civilization, lost its sensitivity as to be practically nil. In Indian and savage tribes, it was extended until it could be used to trail an enemy with accuracy, but today it is only possible to smell something that is within the proximity of the nose. This sense too can be so deceived that a synthetic perfume seems as good and authentic as the actual extract of the flower it represents.

In fact, it is easily fooled, as are all the senses, and it is from these senses, faulty as they now are, that the human mind has gathered all of its vaunted intelligence. It admits that none of the senses are dependable, and yet it will take the findings of these senses as a basis for Truth. No wonder, then, with this faulty concept of how to acquire truth, Jesus said, "The wisdom of man is foolishness in the eyes of God," for man has no intelligent way to acquire real wisdom.

The sense of smell has to do with the breath. When it is properly understood, it will be expanded until it has a capacity again to "breathe the breath of life and become a living soul" in the true sense of the word. It has the power of the Word closely entwined in its capacities and blends readily with the sense of taste.

"He breathed in him the breath of life, and he became a living soul." What kind of a soul was it before it had this sense of smell, if it became a *living* soul the moment it was in-breathed? Answer for yourself.

The "breath of life" carries with it infinite possibilities of attainment, magnificent reaches of manifestation. It is the handmaiden of inspiration. You "inspire," or inhale, or take in Spirit through the functions of smell, and this is what makes the sense of smell loom as so important. Then you are told to flee from that man "whose breath is in his nostrils," for it is going to be deceptive breath and will accomplish nothing but lies and deceit, for it has no other capacity.

Flee from man who judges from the finding of the senses in their unenlightened state.

The Word of Life goes forth on the breath, or goes out into manifestation through the organs of smell. It is strange how we see all of the unen-lightened senses full of errors and reduced to limited activities and how they all take on new and more wonderful proportions the moment we are conscious of their capacity in Spirit. So the sense of smell begins its wonderful world as the Breath of Life bearing the Word. That Word cannot return void, for it has in it this Breath of Life and must become a living entity, a manifest thing with the capacity to carry through to success. Any word that has the Breath of Life is en route to embodiment and must accomplish whereunto it is sent.

"Speak the word, and my servant shall be made alive" — and the Word goes forth on the breath, on the extended sense of smell; it scents its way out to the place of expression. It is able to trail the enemy (evil belief) to his lair — a new and wonderful capacity that is opened up to this sense.

Across the night of life apart from God is breaking the dawn of the New Day. The New Day is brought into full noontide by these marvelous new senses, which at last are being freed from the prison house of thought. Contemplate the wonder of the sense of smell; understand in its further capacity of breath how it is that every word you utter is launched with the Breath of Life. You are breathing into your universe the living, vibrating word. The word that *you* now speak goes on and on and on, and as it passes along, it sustains everything that touches it.

Smell is the power to exhale a wholesomeness and youth which is sensed by everyone who comes near you. Effortlessly does this happen. The Light which is established in you does everything automatically. You do not try anymore to extend any of your senses; they are automatic in action, able to reach out and bring into alignment all that is awry.

From out of the depths of your soul goes an incense that clarifies the air about you and sweetens the atmosphere in which you dwell. All these things that seem so worthless to human thought become vital manifestations to the awakened consciousness.

Once you become conscious, even in a degree, of the new level of expression, you will begin to "do the works." You will dare to do what Jesus instructed you to do—easily, naturally, normally. You will step out onto the waters and arrive this time at the boat, for you will not again go back to the thought-plane of life and find that you cannot possibly do that which you are doing.

So will you breathe the Breath of Life and raise the dead and heal the sick and scatter such an avalanche of blessings that there will not be room to receive them.

You are at the point of giving to every man whatsoever he asketh—and also at the place of interpreting the asking of the unenlightened one in terms that will meet his needs better, perhaps, than the actual thing he is demanding. But all this will come at the moment of need. You will do the right thing; you will say the right word; you will give the right thing, and so on, and every time you have acknowledged the gift, you will increase it.

You are reaching a wonderful state of revelation. New light and substance are coming down into manifestation, for the senses have been extended out into the far country. The border of your tent has been enlarged. It takes in things that formerly came under the head of the mystic and the impossible. As soon as you assume a given state of consciousness, the things that seemed so mystic and unreal therein become real and normal. You immediately shove off into deeper waters. It is a never-ending variety—a ceaseless flow of substance into expression, the River of Life flowing through the garden of your body, watering it with living waters and causing it to bloom in and out of season.

All the former things that could not find a place of expression come into fruition and bear, in and out of season.

You do not have to wait any longer for the manifestation, if you can see this power of the Breath of Life which has entered into you.

As you contemplate this sense of smell in terms of the Breath of Life pouring in and out of the temple, you are filled with amazement; and yet not surprised that the Word, floated out on this Breath of Life, can shatter the most adamant human manifestation that persists in standing in the way of your on-going.

As the waters of Life which Jesus was willing to give to the Samaritan woman were not only to quench her thirst but to become a living fount in the midst of her (had she been able to see), so with the Breath of Life that is in the midst of you. It is the fountain of inspiration. And when this inspiration has come into manifestation in your life, it shall lead you into all things that you have been seeking, lo these many years.

But as in the case of the woman at the well, you fail to perceive. "If you had recognized God's gift, and who it is that says to you," etc. She saw only what she saw, and so nothing else mattered in her life. And she wanted to argue. She already had someone who was greater—she had her father, Jacob. He was greater than this man who could not drink the waters from the well without a rope and bucket with which to draw them. So the old drama goes on.

The Breath of Life is nothing unless it is everything; it is nothing unless it is recognized, and the gift remains nothing unless it is accepted as a gift. Do you begin to "smell" your way through to the place of the most High? Can you scent the glory of His coming with the perfume of Spirit which He sheds about you?

"This is holy ground; take off your shoes." Do you hear?

"Well, I don't see what difference it would make whether I take off my shoes or not. My shoes have soft soles and ..." etc., etc.

"Take off your shoes."

The old human reasoning and understanding must be cast aside if you are to enter in and be saved; if you are to be able to recognize Me when I appear.

The New Day spoken of in the revelation, when the lion will lie down with the lamb, is at hand, for at last, through the revelation of Jesus Christ, are all thoughts brought under subjection. They are finally deprived of all power and have come again into the proper place of obedience. The poison shall be taken from the serpent, and the savageness destroyed in the lion; all the power of thought shall be lifted up to the one Power, and the kingdom divided against itself shall fade into nothingness.

This whole millennium shall take place in the individual. It will all be performed in the consciousness of *you*, the awakened one. The old thoughts and conditions shall be so completely divested of individual power as to become the willing servants of the Master. And the Master shall walk in His garden and be content.

The Master, this Jesus Christ, the perfect union of the body and Soul, shall then be the true temple of the living God and shall show forth the brightness of this Light through the extended senses, which shall pierce the darkness of anything that is still in the night of separation.

You are gradually coming to the point of recognition of this *temple*-body and its power to step down, or bring forth, the works of God. Through all these newly discovered powers of the senses, you shall be able to bring into manifestation the things that eyes (the blinded sense-eyes) could not see and ears (the deafened ears) could not hear, and all the wonderful things that have not yet "entered into the heart of man" because of its being too clogged with emotions and all sorts of beliefs, held for years. The false sense of spirituality shall have passed in favor of *power*, which emanates into expression through these marvelous, extended channels.

"Be still, and know that I am God" becomes a deepening of the consciousness. It becomes an expander of understanding, as you suddenly begin to try your wings and traverse the unexplored part of your new kingdom.

Suddenly you are alive in this new state of Being and are conscious for the first time that you are here to be "about your Father's business," that you are here that God, the Omnipotent, may have a body, or a place of expression, and not remain forever in the unseen. The heaviness of human thought is disintegrating along all lines, and the superfine substance of Spirit, which can penetrate any matter-substance with the ease of light coming through a window-pane, begins to manifest itself. It is all awaiting the command, now that it is in subjection to God.

The thought-stream that flows from this new state of Life is not creative but is merely a means of putting into expression that which is the will of God. And so your will becomes My will, and My will becomes your will, and the will of God is being done. In other words, you are entering into the rest and peace of the people of God. It is the healthy, active rest of expressing this new Power in the fatigueless body, or temple, which now has "become flesh," for the Soul and body are one, and the new substance is able to receive all of the new dimensions of Light pouring over and through it, and the former congestion of human thought is gone.

Like a frozen river in the hot spring sunshine, the old physical conditions and appearances on the outside finally have given place to the temple "not made with hands, eternal in the heavens" — the temple, or body, which is suddenly discovered to be ageless, deathless, and fatigueless.

Once you discover these new senses that have to do with the temple, you will find that their passing through the temple will bring no possibility of fatigue, for there is no more congested matter to become tired. It has been clogged with the poison of generations of human thinking and believing. Now it moves as freely as the substance of Light and performs what it formerly could not accomplish, through the aid of the Power. You are able to "walk and not be weary, and run and not faint."

The beliefs that formerly made your body a wreck, just because it had performed its duty, now pass over it and cause it to function, just as electricity passes into expression through a dynamo. You begin to feel in terms of Light and to hear in terms of Light. You hear the consciousness back of everything.

As you descend into the plane where matter is still dark and heavy, you are able to remain completely above the deception of it. It is impossible for you to be tricked again into accepting matter as a power or as a substance which can resist this Light. You have come to the "touch me not" command to all the former beliefs and are free. Yet will you live in the world but not be of its terrible scourge of human belief.

It is wonderful. All this is to take place by the "gift that is within you" being stirred up and *let* to come into manifestation here and now. You will have to perform all this glorious resurrection yourself. You will have to "pick it up" or "lay it down" as you see fit, for now you have come to the day of Self-expression because you have dropped off "self" expression.

The light of the sense of smell, the glorious breath of the Almighty, pours through you, reviving everything with which it comes in contact. You "smell out" the deep and hidden perfumes of Spirit and are able to give this heavenly aroma to the spoken word so that now it will be sweet instead of bitter. The little book which was "sweet to the taste and bitter to the digestion" has at last been assimilated, and the glorious sustenance of this little book has been discovered to be Life everlasting and perfect, here and now.

"Speak the word." As the sense of smell draws the perfume from the lily, so this extended sense will be able to draw the sweetness out of life; will be able to find sweetness where bitterness has almost obscured it, just as the bee can take the honey from the poisonous flower without getting any of its poison.

"I must be *all things* through Christ, who strengtheneth me." You are all things to all people. You are what you decree yourself to be. You go up and down in the scale of manifestation at will, in order to save "lost sheep." It is too fantastic to be true—that is why it is true.

So you reverse the bluff of human thought which, though a beggar in life, thought to pose as the king, only to be unmasked and cast out. Now you have discovered that you are the child of the King of Kings and were created and sustained by this central infinite Light, God. Everything cometh down from the Father of Light, "in whom is no variableness, neither shadow of turning."

"And he breathed in him the breath of life,
and he became a living soul."

# Chapter XV

# The Sense of Taste

*O taste and see that the Lord is good.*

"Eat my body, drink my blood"—and throw the skeleton away. You do not need that any more after you have eaten My substance and drunk of My inspiration. So you discard and go by the shells and patterns of former things.

You are told to follow Me, the Lord your God, not Jesus; yet until you experience this recognition of Me, you are always looking to a man and calling him good. It is true that Jesus was good and glorious and not to be denied the full recognition for the unparalleled gift He brought to us. Yet in His own language ("Call not me good") and His constant effort to make men see that He was not doing anything of Himself ("Of myself I can do nothing") He was indicating that the skeleton, Jesus as man, must be left behind, and the substance, God or Father, incorporated into the new structure, the new temple that was presently to appear out of the clouds of human belief.

We realize the true sense of taste only when we free it from its limitation of the conscious mind. You can be fooled easily from this standpoint. A synthetic flavor can be passed off as genuine, and your sense of taste will verify it. You do not know whether or not it is genuine, and your taste cannot tell you. So is it with the tasting of various systems of truth and ideas. You cannot tell the synthetic from the real, not even from the standpoint of intellection. There is no way of knowing. You sample it very much as you do wine or tea and find it tastes all right, and so you begin a diet of this personal stuff that finally clogs up your entire system and causes you to fall by the way.

The five senses are given to you for the express purpose of knowing the universe. These senses are the contacts which go out in all directions, like rays of light, and are able, singly or all together, to pierce the densest wall of human belief.

This sense of taste extends through the resurrected body into discrimination. A sense of discrimination comes to you, which begins by deleting the spurious and worthless things that come into contact with your life and selecting those which are of the highest order. Too much time has been wasted by the human intellect trying to find out what is good and what is bad and what is neither. Now comes this sense of discrimination that eliminates all this useless waste of power. The sense of taste extends to the consciousness of taste in life, which is that subtle something that differentiates counterfeit from true; a subtle sense of choosing the right, of being able to discriminate without giving the offense into which the tactless and untutored blunder.

When you understand this spiritual extension of the sense of taste, you are able to taste; that is, you are able to accept the invitation, "Come, eat and drink without price." It is amazing how these senses, when freed from the limitations of human thought, take on their new duties. They all have their glorious especial offices, and yet they all blend into one, just as all the colors of the rainbow are lost in the White Light of Spirit, in which repose all the colors of the spectrum. Because you cannot see them and because you cannot make them appear does not argue anything in favor of your standpoint except your limitation to comprehend the revelation of Light.

The colors are there, just as everything is already there in God, waiting to be brought into visibility. What matter what the mechanics are! You will be able to encompass them easily when you know the law of extension of the five senses. At the precise and exact moment does this operate out of time and space, in a way which cannot be understood through the intellect.

All manifestation takes place through these senses. When you can really taste, you can never go hungry again! And when you can taste, you can drink of the living waters and never thirst again. "If you had asked me, I would have given you to drink of the living waters ... which if a man drink (taste) thereof, he shall never thirst again."

But the human mind is like the woman of Samaria, who could not ask because she did not recognize that there were living waters. She knew only what she could see or grasp through her human mind, and she was hampered by many limitations. She *knew* that the water was in the well, but she also knew that the well was deep and that there was no rope or bucket, so how could this stranger give her to drink?

And so do we go through life, knowing that the well is deep and no bucket is nearby and no rope available and we are thirsty. And so, believing it impossible to slake our thirst, we perish at the open fount of all waters because we do not know how to "taste and see."

"O taste and *see* that the Lord is good." Imagine it! All are invited to taste and see that Life is good, instead of a mixture of good and evil in which you find much more bitter than sweet. Now are you invited to taste and see that the Lord is good. You are actually invited to begin life in the world of heaven-on-earth and to experience all the delectable creations about you. Can you taste and see?

This wisdom all turns into foolishness in the eyes of the thought-taking individual because dust is thrown into his eyes and gall put upon his tongue, in order that the "wise and prudent" shall no longer profane the temple of the living God. The coal of fire is on the lips now for certain, and you are not going to discuss or argue anymore about the Truth. You did not come to destroy, not even silly little beliefs, but to fulfill. And you will know and perceive the futility of trying to tell people something that is wholly false to them. You will "show John," but be sure in this showing you do not get anxious and show off. You show as easily and simply as the dawn breaks, because you can do nothing else, any more than can the dawn when morn arrives.

You *taste* of life not to make others believe in you, but in God. You begin to partake of the heavenly viands that are offered you by the Father within.

The revelation comes, "The kingdom of heaven is come nigh unto you." The kingdom of heaven is a state of consciousness manifested. Formerly, heaven was a state of consciousness unmanifested and was someplace to which you were going and where you were going to be protected from the hell of human difficulties in which you had been stewing all these years. Now the kingdom of heaven is coming nigh unto you. It is sweeping down to the place of manifestation through your extended senses, which are releasing it into the New Age.

The child is to be born, and the command goes forth, "Let the child be born." Do not "try to make" it be born—*let* it be born; let it come forth. "Let there be light: and there was light." Do you begin to sense it? This Power which intertwines itself, which

172

permeates everything in the whole universe, and makes it One?

Is it any wonder, when *you* contemplate this wonderful revelation, that Jesus wept when He heard of some untoward happening which could have been avoided? He did not weep for the person affected. He wept for the futility of His work on this plane. He was sorrowful because, in spite of the long time with His disciples, they did not grasp the significance of being "about my Father's business."

He was not weeping because of any failure of the Power. It was so simple to Jesus that He could not understand why His disciples could not grasp it. He gave every sort of illustration to show them the "how" of it. He put His manifestations in the category of things possible for the child to understand and told them that this same Power was also within them — "The works that I do, ye shall do also, and even greater things than these shall ye do." And yet they would not. They were too buried in the tomb of human beliefs, and only today are we emerging out of this self-created tomb into the light of the New Day.

"My sheep hear my voice," and they will follow after Me, and this Me must be found right in the midst of *you*. It is the Father within you. Your Father is the one who is to call to His sheep and have them respond, and the sheep are the thoughts that have gone wild and astray all these years of mismanagement. Back to you — there is no other place to go now, for there is nothing outside of you that can help or harm you unless you can permit it. You cannot be prospered even by chance unless you can permit it to happen. It makes the human mind furious to hear this, for the one thing it has desired and wanted was to help and prosper itself, and it has tried to do this in a thousand and one ways.

First, it has always been confronted with the problem of a living, not knowing that "man shall not live by bread alone, but by every word that proceedeth out of the mouth of God." Think of it. When you come to this understanding of "tasting," when you begin to taste the word of God and find that it is good and very good, you find it is *all* that is necessary to sustain you. The bread that you work for by the sweat of your brow has no life in it because it is not accompanied by the Word of God. You are to live by the Word of God.

Have you not seen that the Word of God manifests in loaves and fishes? Do you begin to see what this tasting is? How it is that before you have asked, *I* have taken care of this problem of eating which has been so difficult for you? But you would not, because you did not *believe*.

Yet you shall "eat your own words" has been readily accepted by the human intellect. It is never associated with good but with evil. It is never said to a person who is saying beautiful words, "Ye shall eat your own words," but of evil words it is accepted as truth and law.

"Man shall not live by bread alone." It is wonderful when you begin to see this union that is necessary in life before life in its fullness can be comprehended. The leaven and the meal—and then the union, the bread. And so in the Life of you. Presently you will know what it is to bless food or water and change it into *the substance of God manifested.* The reaches of this New Day are so far beyond all thought!

When Jesus addressed the lunatic and was answered in an angered voice, "Go away from us— why do you come here to disturb us?" he demanded to know the lunatic's name.

"Legion is my name, for we are many. If you cast us out, send us away into swine." And so the legion of devilish human thoughts came out and manifested in the loathsome swine, which immediately rushed over the cliff and into the sea of oblivion.

This does not make the pig a loathsome animal any more than it makes Judas a criminal. Both stand as symbols and perform their offices allegorically, as do the rest of the actors in life. But everything is redeemed, and so even the actors who play the violent roles take off their evil human masks when they are ready, and are redeemed. For "there is nothing to be destroyed in all my holy mountain." Finally everything comes to the recognition of its divinity and praises the Lord through its temple, even as you and I.

Again we have the revelation of Jesus at the wedding feast. The human taste had already been deadened by too much drink, but the wine had run low, and they called on Jesus. Why did they call on Jesus? What happens? Does he moralize on drinking? Does he follow the instructions of his host to supply a cheap claret because the taste is dulled? No, he produces the best wine of the entire banquet, but to what end? They could not taste it because they had lost their taste.

And so you begin to see the revelation through the parable. God does not stoop to human subtlety or take account of human frailty when He comes to manifestation. The good wine is just as possible as the sour or bad, and so Jesus, being of the Father degree of consciousness, brought it out. *If a man could taste it, he could; but if he could not, it was there just the same, no matter however much he argued.*

So with Life. It is just the same, no matter what your belief may be. You may argue that you cannot taste it, and that may be true to you; but it does not change the quality of the wine of Life. And so on, down through all the strata of the senses, you can taste only what you can taste and see what you can see. But that does not make anything that you see, taste, etc., of inferior quality because you find it that way. You can find appearing only the degree of your acceptance. You understand? You see? Or can you taste a little and see that life is good—even though you have been dulled by the tasting of inferior foods and of experiences as bitter as gall.

Your name, too, is legion, and so that aggregate mass of beliefs called your history and your human findings must come out of you and be cast into the sea of oblivion. Do you see? Or do you?

All these various illustrations seem to give license, but if they do, it is your mistaken interpretation. All license is a belief in something that is not legal, and so it will be illegal and irregular to you, not natural, and will bring its own reward. But the stepping-up into the Fatherhood degree brings freedom and understanding and balance, a clear vision and tasting of life which enables you to partake of the All-Good quite naturally and regularly and legally. In this realm of Spirit, there are no illegitimate creations. Such can happen only from what you have chosen to call license, while in the next breath you say that everything is created by God. Just what do you believe, anyway? And are you beginning to see that what Jesus said about the foolishness of your wisdom is true and everlastingly true? Do you? Or do you?

"Come out from among them, and be ye separate." Come out from these thoughts that have been piling up about you, in forms so adamant they seem impossible to surmount, and let this stream of revelation flow through them and wash them away.

This revelation enters the temple, and your taste, with its sluggish appetite or its greedy palate, is cleansed and freed from all unlikely foods. Your tasting of life has been made bitter by the poison sea fruits upon which you have been feeding—fruits of the Dead Sea upon which you have tried to live. Now are you sustained and fed by the substance of God in the midst of you.

"Ho, every man that thirsteth, let him come to the waters of life and let him drink." Do you hear this wonderful invitation? The taste has been made sweet and clean. You are beginning literally to "feed among the lilies," and this satisfies you. The dead letter upon which you have been living—the words, systems, ideas, and organizations which you have had to digest in order to get one grain of substance —are all passed away. You are arising and going to your Father-Consciousness, where there is enough and to spare. Enough and to spare? There is ever the fatted calf whenever you can taste it, and it will always be there whenever you can arise and raise all of these lovely senses into the realm of Spirit.

"O taste and see that the Lord is good."

# Chapter XVI

# When You Pray

*Human anguish is the product*
*of the loss by man of his true identity.*
— *Antoine De Saint-Exupéry*

There is something glorious about prayer when it is debunked of all its religious trappings and made to appear for what it is — an actual and literal talking with God. There is something automatically sacred about it that keeps it from the profane, something that saves it from being thrown to dogs and cast before swine.

Yet it can be approached with the same abandon as a great mathematician approaches the principle of mathematics. The more he magnifies and believes in mathematics the deeper he goes into it and the simpler it becomes. A very difficult problem may often be solved very quickly and simply in algebra, which would take endless figuring in lower mathematics. And while all illustrations are more or less futile when we speak of God, yet, in some roundabout way, we conceive that by "magnifying the Lord" within our own consciousness do we automatically come into something which cannot be put into words — but which results in the manifestation of "things hoped for."

There is something glorious about prayer—something filled with light. *When you enter in and shut the door and pray*—what words! What mystery-filled words of Light! When you enter in and shut the door, anything can happen—just as the electrician enters into the closet wherein is kept the great switchboard that controls the water, light, and heat of a great city—in fact, the apparent lifeblood of the city. Do you begin to sense what you do when you enter in and shut the door and then pray? It is not a matter of pulling switches and turning knobs, but the results are far greater and more wonderful.

That is why eventually you will begin to understand that secrecy must preserve thee, and you will automatically withdraw from the talk of and about a thing so precious and wonderful as prayer. Results must and will follow, for when you pray aright, the result exists before the question—just as the answer to every problem is before the problem has been concocted.

The price of a dozen articles at two cents each already is known, even before you put the article up at that price. So, likewise, the exact and perfect answer to your prayer exists before you formulate the question. If the answer did not already exist, then nothing on this earth could cause it to be. Do you see, we are living in a *finished world*—the slow unfolding of it is not the fault of the Truth but of the "glass, darkly" of unbelief through which we have been looking.

There is something nice and freeing about accepting the finished prayer idea—the "before you ask, I will answer; and while you are yet speaking, I will give it unto you—something that takes away all skepticism and fear that you have not made yourself clear to God. There is something reassuring and strength-giving to the acceptance of this fact. Even though the appearances about you testify to the very opposite, and ten thousand proofs of the evil are given to you on every hand, yet will the answer come through into manifestation, if you "pray aright."

There is a lovely sense of freedom, also, which comes when you realize that beseeching and begging are not included in the prayer. The sudden panic that overtakes us wherein we beat our hands and say, "Oh, what shall I do, what shall I do," suddenly gives way to an enveloping Light of the Presence—and the lips are sealed in breathless adoration. For "I will never leave you" is true and real and can come to you and cover you like a cloak of Light—instantly.

In the days of peace and calm, when there is no excitement in the relative world in which you live, prayer is just as effective too; for prayer is not a safety valve for escape from evil but is also for the development or the revealing of your true identity. "Pray without ceasing" is not the anguish of suffering but the constant standing in the Light of the revelation. It is like standing on the mountaintop and experiencing the coming of dawn—light and more light until the full day appears. Thus prayer acts on the darkened senses.

And prayer is a personal, private thing. It is an actual talking with God. Not to a man-god—but a talking which is very much the same as when you suddenly find yourself in the midst of music, with harmony pouring all over and round about you, with melody and glorious, sudden outbursts of surprise and joyous cadences and crescendos.

Yes, prayer is really something.

And prayer is the one thing you can take with you always into any situation; no man can deprive you of the use of this lovely gift. I am so thrilled to be recording all these things from the place of Light to you. It has gone out from this plane of Light, flowing down through the human mechanism, until at this moment it has come to the door of your consciousness.

Do you hear Me knocking this instant at your door? Will you let Me in so that we may break bread? You give Me your problem and I give you the answer. I give you the substance of things hoped for in exchange for the shadows of want and fear that you bring with you. Isn't it wonderful? Do you see?

"Come unto me all ye that labor and are heavy laden, and I will give you rest." I said, "I will," not perhaps or maybe. I said "I will"—that is, if you can accept it. So enter into your closet and "ask the

Father in secret, and he shall reward thee openly." Do you believe?

"Now Solomon, when he had made an end to prayer, the fire descended from heaven and consumed the burnt offering, and the glory of the Lord filled the house."

There is something fine also about making an end of praying. It predicates assurance that you have acted with integrity and belief. There is something fine in loosing the prayer so that it can go out like a homing pigeon and encircle the world and come back with its olive branch of manifestation. "It is done" — an air of finality surrounds all true prayer, just as the dark earth encircles the seed which has been cast into it.

Yes, there is something clean and fine and filled with integrity about making an end to prayer — like relaxing into a sound, dreamless sleep from which you awaken renewed and restored and of which you exclaim, "I slept well." How did you know you slept, if you were asleep? You were never asleep, but the tired, fretting human thing that had gotten itself into a turmoil was quieted until the reinforcements necessary to victory could be brought into manifestation.

Do you see how it is that the integrity of prayer causes you to wait patiently for Me to bring out the manifestation which seems so impossible at the moment.

There is something majestic in making an end to prayer—a kingly something which knows that "My words are spirit, and they are truth," and they "shall not return unto me void, but shall accomplish whereunto they are sent." You can almost see the glorious declaration of prayer go forth into the great cosmos, causing a sudden integration to take place which will materialize and be made flesh.

Prayer of recognition might be likened to a magnet of any shape which was placed in the neighborhood of steel filings. Instantly the attraction is set up, and the filings which are to form the shape of the magnet come into alignment automatically and as if by magic. The moment the matrix, or pattern, is presented to the Presence, it is filled with the unseen substance. It needs only recognition of this fourth-dimensional Jesus Christ Consciousness to solidify it into manifestation.

All this a child can do, but an adulterous adult cannot—because he just knows that it cannot happen. It is something that has to take place. Even God could not change the action of His own laws since He is changeless as far as things of Spirit are concerned. The only place of change is in the human consciousness or thought. Today you dislike some thing or person, tomorrow you like both of them—and so it goes. But not so with the law of God. It cannot be changed, broken, added to, or taken from. It is the foundation of all our hopes, dreams, and desires.

And "having done all, stand, and see the salvation of the Lord." This is the thing which makes the human thought panicky, for after having made an end to prayer, it would take up again the old tedium of looking at appearances.

It is not unlike sister Anne in the tale of "Bluebeard." She is working against fearful odds. There may be moments or hours of what appears to be vacuity, followed by hours of super-abounding joy; hours of neutral, colorless—yea, meaningless nothing. But when you have *actually prayed*, there is always something underlying it which causes you to hold on, a sort of consciousness that things are going on underneath.

But one cannot make an end to praying unless he has prayed aright. If he is still beseeching God to do something which he considers a miracle, he is sure of defeat, for the manifestation of the God-Power is no miracle to God—it is natural. And since God is going to do the work, it rests entirely with Him, and the manifestation rests with you—your willingness to *let* it through in the way of God's appointing and not after the manner of some man.

Looking for results according to your own limited concept of things is merely to return to the human thought and causes more beseeching and begging and the making of long word-prayers to a man-god.

Most prayer is a sort of bargaining with God—a pitiful offer to give God something in return for a miracle. "When you are ready, *I* will do the work" is the answer to all that. If you are not ready, you cannot have the works done in you, and the being ready is nothing in this world but a complete surrendering of your own personal ideas and beliefs.

God is not pleased with tribute money since all the wealth of the universe is in His hands; and He is not pleased with the blood of rams and goats and pigeons. Imagine the Lord of the universe being pleased or displeased because you did or did not eat caviar during Lenten week? Why, it sounds like something out of *Alice in Wonderland!* Then imagine the joy over one sinner being saved—one more avenue for this glorious Light to come through. That is all that takes place when a sinner is saved. A new avenue or temple has been opened for the Light of God to shine through, and you, the temple, do not care how much it floods out through the portals and windows of your church.

Isn't it glorious! You see the temple of the living God, and the Light of this God is flooding through your house!

So you awaken to the Fear of God—because you have cleansed your temple of the *fear* of God. Everything is reversed, and everything you are told to do, you are immediately told not to do. That is where the understanding comes into manifestation. Praise the Lord. It is wonderful and glorious.

When the real Fear of the Lord comes to you, it is understood to be the reverence of the Power. You would no more think of attempting to misuse this Power than you would try to misuse electricity. Your fear, or reverence, for this Power would only be natural and normal, and this would take away the fear of the Lord—the ignorance of His power—and you would have progressed out of the state of consciousness which looks for a miracle and would have entered into the place of the natural, normal functioning of the laws of God.

God is like nothing on the earth, for He is All, and this precludes the making of idols to Him. He is not like any power known to man, for He is All-Power. The only monument God ever created as a testimony to His active Power is man—and the resurrection of the temple as a place of God-expression was the mission of Jesus Christ. "Man has worked out many inventions," many of which have or can destroy him, but Jesus came to show how the temples could be resurrected through the offices of true prayer.

Man is busy looking into the archives of yester-day to see if God left some monument or some secret sign on the earth, and thousands apparently have found something; but one by one they are proven to be the monument in which is contained all things, even the prophecy of the end of all flesh—the temple-body of man. When you begin to see this even vaguely, you will begin to understand why He "went within and shut the door" whenever He wanted to find out anything. Affirmation made therein from the "it is done" state of consciousness will immediately have its confirmation. The "two shall agree, and it shall be established on the earth."

I suppose you tried when you were a child to curry special favors from "teacher" by an occasional bunch of violets or a red apple. I know I did, and sometimes it worked amazingly; I have known of one bunch of violets to jump a grade ten points in a single month. But God is no teacher, and He has all the violets to begin with, to say nothing of the red apples—and He is not moved. No, the beseeching, begging, telling God all sorts of nice truths about Himself avail nothing—but sudden recognition of the Presence opens up a whole new field of expression.

It is so wonderful—I have to keep reminding you of it all. I know you know it, but when I am writing, I get so thrilled that I am writing to you and that perhaps it has only this instant become real to you. Of course, you have known it for ages, but this is refreshing your mind.

Considering all things, the savage in his manner of prayer has a much finer conception—at least he is not a hypocrite when he makes his prayer or oblation to a tree-god. He makes an end to his praying, lays his offering at the feet of his god, and having fulfilled his part of the bargain, goes free— gloriously free. Yet when the civilized man has fulfilled what he thinks is his duty toward God, he then is beset with such worry and wondering that he is driven to all sorts of devices to see whether God is going to keep His part of the bargain. "If ye believe" does go beyond mere credulity. Even the savage believes in what he is doing and hence has a measure of confidence in results.

Do you begin to see why Solomon, the symbol of wisdom, "the soul," made an end of praying? He must have believed. Do you?

And then there is Jesus. When He prayed, He started with, "Thank you, Father" — a full recognition and acceptance of the finished prayer before it was asked. What a lovely sense of abandon comes with such confidence in God. "Fear not" and "I am with you always" take on such power as to lift you actually so that you will not "dash your foot against a stone."

Have you ever thought about the fact that man is the only creation of God that is able to pray? He is the only creature which has choice and power to change the pictures of his life, and he has been given full instructions as to how this is done. Yes, you have been given the "open sesame" to the kingdom of heaven, and whether you accept this and "arise and go" unto this level of consciousness, or sit in the pigsty complaining about the awful lot which has been yours, is entirely up to you.

A dog has no such chance. He has nothing better than an instinct to carry him through. You have the glorious Word of God Almighty. You have been told the Secret, and yet, hypnotized by the appearances which you have accepted as real, you do little better than respond to a kind of dulled instinct, which in many cases is not as intelligently used as that of a dog—bringing upon your head such ugly admonitions as, "Go to, thou sluggard, consider the ant," and a little more gentle but nonetheless firm, "Consider the lilies."

Look about you and see that all the lesser manifestations of life are protected and taken care of, but you have the freedom of choice and the freedom to move into higher and higher levels until you have completely returned to the Father-Consciousness (house), wherein you find yourself created in the image and likeness of God, a little lower than the angels.

Lost in the consciousness of wanting things and trying to make God change His mind or do your bidding, you are still wondering whether prayer "works" or not. It does not and never did, for prayer is not some trick of the human mind which causes God to jump about like a jumping-jack and accomplish your bidding.

Prayer is the sure and certain alignment with power, which causes you and your slow-thinking apparatus to take on a new level of expression, just as a man walking beside a fast-moving streetcar might suddenly jump on. Though he remains perfectly still, yet he is carried along at many more miles per hour than he can possibly go by his own effort.

Prayer is like that—suddenly you are picked up, and at the moment of contact, you are swept along into new levels wherein you discover the answered problem instead of the way to work it out.

Do you begin to see why you are to "be still, and know that I am God"—instead of telling Me all about it and trying to go over all the details of your life and needs, when "your Father knoweth that ye have need of these things." Don't waste any more time in the subterranean passages of the human concept of prayer. "Come unto me and be saved." Isn't it wonderful when you see it?

No matter how far afield you find yourself— probably you have been in and out of half a dozen organizations, lauded them to the skies and then reduced them to dust, always complaining of what they wanted to do to you in the final analysis.

They didn't want to do anything to you that you did not invite in the first instance. How? Why, simply by accepting them as true. What you accept comes to abide with you as a truth, and what you reject passes you by. Understand? And so the awful fear that you brought out of some of the organizations or personal teachers has no more power than you have given it. The moment you break the supply lines, it or they move out of your field of activity. Even the place thereof shall be no more. Understand?

Finally I think you will hear Me when *I* say unto you, "Follow thou me." That is simple and clear enough for a child—too simple for you perhaps, but after you have gotten over some of your higher learning, you may return unto Me and be saved from the awful confusion of many minds. There is only one Mind, but be sure somebody or some organization does not convince you that the infinite Mind has been crowded into the skull bone of a little man or woman or the somewhat larger place of an organization.

Have you ever had such wonderful invitations as, "Lean on Me;" "Cast your burdens on Me, and *I* will sustain you." (*I will*—not maybe or perhaps, but *I will* sustain you.) It's too good to be true; it's too wonderful—and yet it is true.

The human sense is so muddled by its accumulated beliefs in a two-power universe and a separate existence that it cannot possibly see how the law operates, and so it continues bargaining with God, offering something it thinks is worthwhile for a much larger return. One minute it half-heartedly believes that something is going to happen; the next it is peeping to see if there are any signs. The worst of it is that nothing is going to happen, and the interesting part of it is that the one making that kind of prayer will wind up by saying, "Well, I never did believe there was anything to it." And by that admission, he has proven the power of prayer, for he got exactly what he believed would happen—nothing.

"The measure (motive) you mete ... ." It makes no difference what the outward show or what the words may be—it is the *motive* behind it. A woman came to me for help. She wanted to recover five thousand dollars which she said she had given to an organization five years before, when she was in the fury of its teaching. "But," I said, "you never really gave it, or else you would not be trying to get it back now. Your motive at that time was an investment; your outward manner was a gift. You lost, for God is not a stock exchange."

The fact of the matter was that the woman got huge praise and flattery when she made the gift, and basked in the adulation. She was pointed out as a real Christian, etc., and she fed plenteously on that sweet treacle, enjoying more than five thousand dollars' worth of praise and approbation.

The *motive* you mete to the universe—be careful what the motive is because you might find yourself asking a little later for your gift which was no gift. "When ye pray," be careful for what you pray, what the real thing is back of your asking, for that is coming to pass.

I just heard a very saccharine voice, dripping with holiness, telling of the "love-offering plan." I wondered about the motive back of it. Usually you can tell from the tone of the voice whether it is *Love* offering or love offering—you know what I mean, don't you?

There is something fine and clean about the Consciousness that actually goes ahead about its Father's business and knows, actually and fearlessly, that "the laborer is worthy of his hire" and that the gift will and must be "laid upon the altar." Don't you think so? And that is not offering any criticism whatsoever of the love offering. For when the heart is full of gratitude for the blessings received, that gratitude must pour over into expression. "Your Father knoweth that ye have need of these things"—so stop trying to *make* them appear through any given channel and *let* Me come in and break bread with you. Understand? I believe you do.

Once you get the idea that *Life* is self-sustained and that life must be sustained, then you will see just what is meant by "man shall not live by bread alone, but by every word that proceedeth out of the mouth of God." Life is self-sustained, and if you can blend *your* life with it, you too will be self-sustained and shall have plenty of actual bread which will proceed out of the Word—which proceedeth out of the mouth of God. Understand?

I think you do. I think you are beginning to see that the duality is being picked up and made One and that the point of connection is prayer, that golden umbilical cord which connects God and His manifestation. It is just wonderful. Prayer is that golden lane of light connecting the shadow with its substance; connecting your physical body with the real man, "made in the image and likeness."

When you stay too long in the thought-world of the shadow matter-body, you become involved with its laws and get into a web of self-hypnotism. You begin working with little success against the appearances of evil that you have induced by this apparent separation, and then suddenly you return unto Me and are saved. In other words, you return to the original, changeless Permanent Identity, and immediately the shadow changes likewise. Understand? I think you are beginning to see just what true prayer really is. "The perfect picture shown to you on the mount" is what you see, and then the shadow of that perfection is recast if it has slipped out of alignment.

The scales will fall from your eyes, and you will see and know that there is an end to praying for the glory it brings you personally. You will be through selling prayers. You will find yourself praying without ceasing because you cannot do otherwise than recognize the Presence of God here, there, and everywhere. You cannot help doing good and healing and helping because it is your very nature to do these things automatically, and anybody who touches you in the crowds of Life will receive the healing—the virtue will go out of you whether you know it or not.

Understand? I think so. See the difference between the attitude of true prayer and praying for a love-offering or the approbation of man. Do you see?

"Now, Solomon, when he had made an end to prayer, the fire descended from heaven and consumed the burnt offerings, and the glory of the Lord filled the house."

Notice the fire did not descend from heaven until he had made an end to praying. He had finished—the contract had been signed, sealed, and delivered; the agreement made and oneness established. And then—why, then the fire descended from heaven and consumed the burnt offerings—burned up all the shapes and forms, mental and physical, of the limitations which had been keeping him from his sense of heaven here and now. Automatically and directly, you finally have come to the end of your praying. When you have accepted the Real and True, then something happens, and you see the symbol of purification manifesting.

And then the glory of the Lord fills the house (consciousness), and you find yourself in the courts of the Lord, the courts of Light and Revelation. The glory—that indescribable word—the glory of the Lord fills the house, and you have a deep sense of peace and revelation that cannot be put into words.

Yes, Beloved, when ye pray, make an end to it because you actually believe—and then rest in silence and feel the fires descending upon your earth, burning out every appearance of evil. After this wonderful cleansing of the Spirit, experience that most wonderful glory of the Lord filling the

house— your house, your consciousness. Do you
believe? I believe you do.

# Chapter XVII

## An Invitation

An invitation came in one day from a very interesting speaker. It said something to the effect that "Miss Blank" would give a series of Sunday lectures; that she would be under the influence of a noted orator who had long since passed over.

I went to that lecture because I knew that the group connected with it were people of integrity and sincerity. I took with me an open mind, and this is what happened:

A frail little woman came up on the platform. She was nervous, evidently unaccustomed to public speaking or appearance. She fidgeted about in her chair while the preliminaries were going on, and when called upon to speak, she arose as shyly as a schoolgirl giving her graduation talk.

What she said by way of self-introduction was quite sketchy, spoken in a most uncultured, high-pitched voice. It was something to the effect that she was not accustomed to speaking in public and had little or no education (all of which was quite obvious) but that her guide (naming the deceased orator) would address the audience through her.

Then a "miracle" happened.

The moment she let go of her own personality, she straightened up into an authoritative posture, looked fearlessly at her audience, and began a speech, in cultured and perfect English, that held one from beginning to end. It was a speech on Power and one that almost any speaker would have been proud to have originated or delivered.

The easy, well-modulated voice poured out of the mouth of that woman who had just said in untutored tones that she was incapable of giving a lecture on her own initiative! It was as perfect a demonstration of the law of Jesus Christ as I have ever known. The moment the little unlettered, uncultured mortal-concept stepped aside, in rushed the glorious Permanent Identity to carry on in the manner described.

Jesus was an unlettered boy, yet we find Him in the temple teaching men steeped in erudition. You do not think for a moment that Jesus, the carpenter boy, had anything to say to learned doctors, do you? But at the same time, He had everything to say to them—through this inner Lord. Did He find Himself in difficulties, He immediately "went unto the Father," and then things happened that could not take place through the Jesus of the third-dimensional plane.

The law for becoming a successful lecturer is indicated as follows: "You do not need to think what you are going to say; open your mouth and I will supply the words." Do you believe that? Well then,

199

you understand how Jesus, the untutored boy, could instruct the doctors and how it is possible for you to do the same in that or any field you elect since "the works that I do, ye shall do also, and even greater works shall ye do, because I go unto my Father." Do you believe that?

Do you begin to see, then, why Jesus counseled, "Judge not from appearances, but judge righteous judgment"? Do you begin to see how everything that the little speaker with the untutored voice said about herself was not true about her Self? And that the moment she was able to sidestep this "conscious" personality, she was free from all its limitations?

The same is true of the pictures of disease and failure. All these evils and many more reside in the conscious-thinking mind and have their residue in the subconscious mind, the storehouse of memory; and as the old song goes, "Memory is the only thing that grief can call its own," so it is the only thing by which you can perpetuate evil in your life. For the moment the mental picture is blacked out or the thought broken, the picture on the body disintegrates; the limitation is moved away, the obstacle melts into nothingness, and the highway of our Lord, the Father within, is made straight—just as the moment the film in a projecting machine is snapped or cut, at that instant the screen shows forth again blank and ready for another picture, and without mar or mark of all the tragedies and other experiences that have raced over it.

So it is with you. Just the moment the thought is broken, the former pictures which apparently have made such inroads into your body and havoc in your life are no longer; and the effects of former thoughts are also invisible, for they were only shadows of human thinking thrown upon an otherwise perfect man (-ifestation) or screen.

If you can hide behind a mask on the stage, you feel quite comfortable because the limitations of your personality are gone. So if I choose to play L'Aiglon behind a mask of greasepaint, I am freed from the limitations of John Smith. Imagine some of the personalities who have essayed the roles of swashbuckling kings and queens with ease and talent, who came from under the mask of greasepaint and returned to their small hall bedrooms with nothing better than a cold supper for the erstwhile "king" or "queen."

Do you begin to see how Jesus saw this "liar and the father of it" (mortal mind) for what it was worth? He knew that it was nothing, a mirage, and could be changed at a moment's notice. That is why "in the twinkling of an eye, all shall be changed."

But nothing that is real can be changed, so all that is changed is the thought and the shadow-pictures that seem so real and true and backed up by concrete testimony. These are changed slowly or "in the twinkling," in accordance with your ability to appropriate the Light. That too, then, is why you are told to "be still, and know that I am God."

How beautifully this Light is breaking over the universe again, and now it is finding open doors and windows and is flooding through everything, revealing the kingdom of heaven here and now. Praise God from whom all (do you hear? *All*) blessings flow. That *all* includes all the desires of your heart, and right here again Spirit recalls to you that "I shall give you the desires of your heart."

Can you take them when they come? Or will you shyly back away from them, advising the world that you are not a speaker and never knew how to speak? Answer me. How long will you walk in the way of the transgressor? Long we have thought of the sinner and the transgressor as those who broke Sunday school laws, but the sinner and the transgressor are those who continue to attempt to break the law of God, the law that was breathed into them in the beginning, establishing them as made "in the image and likeness of God," "a little lower than the angels" and having dominion over everything.

> "Awake thou that sleepest, and Christ shall give thee light." Awake and arise from the dead belief of this thing which is binding you.

I am not discounting the speaker earlier referred to. If it was her idea and accepted belief about how the works she was doing so beautifully were done, it is not my place to offend her by refusing her testimony. I only choose to stand by the fact that there is only *One*, and no matter whether you call It God, Allah, Buddha, or what, makes no funda-mental difference.

Do you begin to understand the tolerance that comes as you journey along the way of Light? You see all the varying degrees of light, but you do not have to bother about anything but the seeker who comes directly to you and asks for help. Then can you fling open wide the doors of your soul; then can you project this white Light to such a degree that all the shadows and limitations of the other's human thought are dissipated.

"What is that to thee?" It is nothing and it is everything, for every time you are able to reduce a manifestation to its common denominator, you are able to return to the one living God and auto-matically set aside human thought-processes which keep you under the curse of the (man-made) law. "With the coming of the law came sin into the world." What will you do with that? It is something to think about for a moment, something to take into the inner shrine and find the Light through which it operates on this glorious plane of the New Day.

So you stand before your audience, no matter whether it is only your family or your office or on the streets of life, and you present a trembling, fearful picture of yourself, making apologies for everything and trying to get the world to accept the fact that your shortcomings and beliefs are true. Yet the moment they agree with you—and naturally, they do—you are angry with them, for fundamentally you do not believe what you have saddled on yourself. If you did, you would stop trying to get rid of your afflictions—would accept them as irremediable.

You see how the Light is undermining every last bit of foundation of evil until finally there will be left not one stone upon another. They shall all be thrown down until the headstone of the corner becomes the keystone of the arch; and that foundation, keystone, cornerstone, of your structure is Jesus Christ—the Word made flesh and the *flesh* made Spirit—and the full and absolute recognition of God in the flesh is made on earth.

As Jesus merged into his Fatherhood degree of Life, so you will step out of your human limitations to find yourself functioning in a new dimension. There you will find a lovely sense of well-being where formerly you had met *dis*-ease, and a wealth of substance where there had seemed naught but vacuity. From this recognition of *your* Father within and the ability to become one with Him, you will be able to sense why Jesus said, "I can of mine own self do nothing," but ...

That was what the timid little speaker said, and that is what you say. But instead of completing the recognition, you are prone to stop on the negative side of it and therefore only make your situation that much worse, for you get accumulated agreement from all the race-consciousness which believes in failure.

So you, as did Jesus, must *push on* into the "but with God all things are possible," for as you do, you "come boldly to the throne of grace" and are deluged with the Light of revelation, which so opens your eyes that you now see the possibility of doing what your Jesus-Consciousness could not accomplish. At long last, you see because your eyes have suddenly become open on this fourth-dimensional plane, and from that elevation, the mystery now is how in the world the eyes of John Smith did not see the kingdom of heaven all about him!

So many words seem necessary to convey this beautiful and simple truth, and while much of it seems like repetition, in reality it is not.

Presently you will feel this incoming tide of Light, experience a quickening, a rising feeling, a stirring within, as the tide mounts higher with each fresh wave and impulsion sweeps you onto the crest of understanding. Charge it off to whatever you like, it makes no difference. The main thing for you to know is that by getting away from the John Smith, you enter into the Christ-Consciousness, the place of Power; and then the temple of John Smith becomes the "stepper-down" of the new revelation.

"Before I can get into the pool, another always steps down." Who is that other? He too is a cripple or an otherwise afflicted person who has, however, to some degree "arisen" into the next dimension.

And such will continue to "step down" (get the idea of stepping-down the Power) in advance of you as long as you stay in the John Smith consciousness, which says to the world, "Well, you see, I cannot speak," or words to that effect. And the world waits a moment to see whether you are going to add "but" and then speak in spite of what you have declared about your human self. Or else the world will tell you none too gently, "Well, if you cannot speak, get down from the platform and give place to another who can," and you bemoan, "Another always steps down ahead of me."

Now, all this seems to imply a race for success in accomplishment, but in reality there is no race, for your prize is already yours.

Yes, you will speak, sing, dance, play, work, or what you will, as soon as you reach the point of knowing that it is the Father within that doeth the works and not the limited John Smith (who has already admitted that he is a hopeless mess as far as expression is concerned). So you go instantly, with your problem or desire, to the Father because by now you have come to the point of acceptance of "He is there in the midst of thee" and "before you ask, I have answered."

You go quickly. "I will ask my Father," and the answer is more enlightening and true than any from the most erudite person in the world. So think of the priceless gift that Jesus gave to you—the knowledge that you (yes, you) could ask the Father, the one and only unfailing authority on any subject, the one and only source of all-mighty power, the one door of the impossible.

"I will ask my Father." What a priceless secret and divine formula you are hearing again! You have the power and ability to ask your Father, and He answers before you ask and is willing and ready to fulfill His promises into visibility. Do you see?

"Ask whatsoever you will." "Heretofore you have asked for nothing; now ask, that your joy may be full." It is wonderful, the glorious revelation! "O taste and see that the Lord is good." "Ho, every man that is athirst, let him come," and he that is an hungered, and "let him drink of the waters of life freely."

Do you see what a magnificent thing you have appropriated—the ability to "ask the Father" and receive the perfect solution to any problem, the divine remedy for any ill? Believest thou this? It is so, and so it is.

# Chapter XVIII

## The Exegesis of God

Jesus is the exegesis of God. An exegesis is defined as "the process of solving an equation," and symbolically, that is exactly what Jesus is and does. He solves the enigma of the human mind and its false creation. He is the Light that came into a world of human confusion and darkness, "the voice of one crying in the wilderness" of human theories and teachings. That magnificent Mind that operates as a go-between for the unseen and the seen is the identical Mind which He invites you to let be in you. "Let that mind (that identical Mind) be in you which was also in Christ Jesus." You then become the solver of the equation of the human mind, which is presented to you in a thousand and one masks of evil.

The more you contemplate Him the greater He apparently grows in stature. You become acquainted with His infinite nature. The contemplation of this causes many of the laws of that Mind to automatically function within you. By the contemplation of this magnificent idea, you find that ideas have already taken place and that you are discovering them in operation. It is like voyaging into an unknown country—new cities appear. They have always been there; you are discovering them, not creating them nor yet causing them to appear. You are automatically putting into effect the power of *recognition*.

And so it is with the various mansions "in my Father's house." They have always been there. You are just moving toward them; eventually you are *absorbed* into the city you so recently saw as a dark spot on the horizon. So are you automatically one with the new mansion, the new state of consciousness which you have recognized. From that moment, you function automatically *from that level*.

Just as a starving man, once filled with food, cannot imagine the pangs of hunger any longer because he no longer has the capacity to be hungry, so is it with man when he enters the consciousness of God; he cannot experience, *has not the capacity* to experience, the belief of lack, disease, or limitations he so recently knew as his heritage. Where does it all go? Like the mirage in the desert, it goes nowhere. The change has been made in the elevation of consciousness.

As you begin to *see*, you also begin to *hear*. One of the subtle changes that takes place is that Jesus Christ becomes the *present tense*.

Presently, you will see why so much prayer is apparently not answered. It is because it is always addressed to something in the past or something in the future. When you identify yourself with that Mind which is also in Christ Jesus, you will discover that all stories and illustrations, and even miracles, become present tense and actually operate in your daily life.

All this seems imaginary and hypothetical to the human thought and is worthless on that level since it cannot be proven. But this does not gainsay that you cannot do so. You learn presently how highly important the silence is. You begin to think in terms of the Presence instead of a dead, historical character. "This is life eternal, to know me" becomes clear and understandable.

Nothing is destroyed in your life but by the fires that you have lighted. Remember, nothing happens but My Love allows—and see the sudden, new orientation take place. The judging, the condemnation, the questioning will cease. You will have the answer before the question, for now you know where the answer lies. You have Him who is speaking to you, *at this instant,* within you.

And so you enter in, close the door, and come to that place of "take no thought." Then—ah, then the floods of etheric energy pass from God into the heart of you with the fleetness of a driven deer. You are chained by fate no longer. You are a *new* creature— the "born again" one. This discovery, through the consciousness of Life, reveals to you your true identity and will lead you into all things. Yes, "This is life eternal; to know Me," your true Self.

You discover that all the evils of your life are the direct result of the divine energy being released negatively through your belief in a dual power. Fear, then, is transmuted into reverence. Thus you are released from the "fear of the Lord" (a tyrant) into the "Fear (awe) of the Lord," which is truly the beginning of wisdom. The negative energy which is released through judging from appearances or accepting the ancestral teachings whips itself into a fury that will eventually destroy you, so terrible does it become, unless it is unmasked.

There is only one panacea for all this, and that is the law of Love. "Perfect love casteth out fear" —and is the only thing which never fails.

So much of the difficulty of life comes from the misunderstanding of desire—and not from the desire. "I shall give thee the desires of thy heart" removes all doubt about desire. Desire is really the thing in its incipiency, pressing toward you for expression, and not something that must be worked out. It is something to be accepted. The reason you have the desire is that the hour has struck when the fulfillment of that desire should take place. The capacity to accept this wonderful truth has been so distorted and prostituted by ways and means of making God do something personal for you that the actual desire and its fulfillment have been diverted into other channels.

Generally, when a desire appears on the horizon of the mind, emotion takes over, and the urgency of the wish or desire becomes so insistent it literally crowds the manifestation out of the pictures. "Be not anxious" is one of the very real laws of God, for when you are anxious or emotional about the fulfilling of the Word of God, you drop a veil of human disbelief. When you attempt to put the clumsy, human "thought-fingers" in to assist the birth, you bring forth a stillborn idea. A "cloud without rain" is the result of this insistence which you call "work."

Jesus said *only* believe. That seems so simple, but when the human mind, with its mad desire to possess, gets into action, the simplicity of it moves out of the picture. The terrible struggle ensues; the all-night fight with the angel is re-enacted. It is all of no use. Until you believe, you might as well return to Egypt and accept the fate pattern of your human life. There is no possibility of grafting the Consciousness of God onto the human mind.

"The weakling can never realize the Immortal." This ancient Upanishad sounds very much like Jesus saying, "Leave all and follow me."

Some think to *use* the truth. Occasionally you hear people who say they have "given up the truth." How can anyone give up the truth? When you *know* the Truth, It becomes *you*, and you can no more separate It from yourself than take the yeast from the bread. Once it has baked, the whole mass becomes a third substance. When we hear of one giving up the truth, we know they are only speaking of a *system* of truth or a personal concept of it.

The brief candle of life becomes the Light Immortal when we touch the Truth, and it can no more be snuffed out by human opinions. The prayers of the righteous "soar incense-like to greet the sky." There is the blending of soul and God, never to be separated again, for the thought of separation has been consumed away.

A fish will never drown in water—neither will a man ever die, as long as he is conscious of having his being in God. If you could only believe, as Jesus has said, you would begin to read in the present tense and in the Presence. You would then *hear* and *experience* such things, literally and symbolically, as "He satisfieth thy mouth with good things, so that thy youth is renewed as an eagle's." These actual transformations are so and can take place when your eyes are opened. This opening of the eyes is not going to be a psychic event but a very normal physical, as well as a spiritual, experience.

Yes, you are the exegesis—the *process* (embodied) of solving and dissolving the problem.

# Meditations

# Blessed Are the Pure in Heart

*Blessed are the pure in heart, for they shall see God.*

Yet you are told "no man shall see God and live." So it would seem that to become pure in heart would be to experience death, and that is exactly what must and does happen.

The moving into the purity of the consciousness of Oneness causes almost daily death. Paul said, "I die daily," for each day, he moved into a more pure or more conscious state of recognizing God. We are not especially concerned with the ordinary meaning of the word *purity* except in the sense that it means singleness, unmixed with foreign ingredients.

When we become single (pure) in purpose, we begin to *see* God. We die, and sometimes we die daily, for we are advancing into a more and more pure recognition of the Presence. As we see God to a greater and greater degree in everything, we begin to look through the human thought-pictures and to detect what is the nature of the congestion that is causing the evil. "I saw you under the fig tree," and so did thousands of others—but I *saw* you, and that is the sight of the one who is *pure*—or single in purpose and belief in God.

Do you begin to see, when we dispose of gods many and minds many, how it is that we begin to experience the purity of Consciousness and we die to the impure state we are in. And as we press forward to the high calling in Christ Jesus, we shall be born again many times, each time to a higher elevation of Life, singleness, purity.

Many people profess to believe in God—but presently you find them running hither and yon because they have heard of a new teaching that might help. Aren't you absolutely sure where you stand at this moment? Do you look for another, or is this "He that should come? You answer.

# The Poor in Spirit

*Blessed are the poor in spirit,*
*for they shall inherit the kingdom of heaven.*

Seems such a contradictory sort of statement since God is Spirit, and so we see that until the words of man are forced to give up their meaning we are confused and dumbfounded. To be poor in spirit, according to the best interpretation of the word, is to be lacking in the stiff-necked pride of the human mind. The high-spirited, stiff-necked being who thinks he is superior to the rest of his race; the intellectual giant who is so sure of his mental superiority, etc. — all this is the *spirit* which is spoken of, and until a man is "poor" in this, he cannot possess the kingdom of heaven.

Spiritual wickedness is the spirit of personal power, either because of fear-teaching or by place and temporal power, and this one cannot enter into the kingdom of heaven, for he is rich in the spirit of worldly power. He can prove his ground until the day of reckoning, and then — well, then he finds he has his mentality stuffed full of this stiff-necked spirit of man's wisdom but lacks the Spirit necessary to save him from his own shortcomings.

When man becomes poor in spirit, he begins to be rich in *Spirit*. As the "ye must decrease, I must increase" takes place, he experiences the freedom of being poor in spirit and rich in *Spirit*.

# The Avenging Angel

*I am the Avenging Angel.*
*I bring not peace, but a sword.*

I am the sword of Damocles, suspended by a hair above the head of the evil one who seeks to destroy you, no matter what its shape or name may be. The moment you *see* what is going on, the evil one, though she parade in garments of Light, has to carry on her reign under a suspended sword, only held by a hair. When she sees this, it will, as it did in the case of Damocles, dispel all the joy of life.

"Blessed art thou when men shall revile you and say all manner of evil against you." Once the scandalmonger has revealed herself by cursing you with her criticism, even though she be the high priestess of some altar, she has caused you to be blessed by recognizing the Christ in you and is then ready for her blessing—and what a blessing! When she finds her arm (power) withered away because she has tried, through her jealousy, to steady the arc of another's soul, she then has time to think it over, and it may be eons of time before she again has the use of that arm (power).

Yes, "the wrath of man shall bless thee," because that wrath is only stirred up because of the jealousy of the Christ in you. Once you see this, you will "bless all those who curse you and do despiteful things"—and incidentally, you will *take* your blessing, for the wrath of man *shall* (not maybe or perhaps) bless thee. Be sure to get your blessing out of it all.

"No (not any) weapon that is formed against thee shall prosper." And most certainly not the tongue of a scandalmonger. Why? "Because thou hast put thy trust in me." Because you have discovered the Permanent Identity encased in the impervious armor of God—yea in a sword, bullet, and word-proof armor.

"I bring not peace, but a sword," the two-edged word of God, turning in all directions, which will decapitate the evil belief and anything that persists in projecting it. Yes, it shall drop in its ignominy— uncoffined, unknelled, and unsung. The evil thing has suddenly been caught in the snare it laid for another.

"Those that are incensed against thee shall be put to shame." I am the Avenging Angel, avenging because the evil can get no farther and turns upon itself with accelerated force and destruction. When the javelin of the Avenging Angel is cast, it pierces the heart of the sturdiest oak of human evil and deceit and vibrates as a golden harp of victory.

"Put up your sword." "Ye do not need to fight … stand and see the salvation of the Lord." Put up your little human sword of trying to prove you are right or the other wrong.

Ye do not need to fight. The Avenging Angel will do all that is necessary. "Vengeance is mine; I shall repay, saith the Lord." So fret not yourself because of evildoers. *I* am the Avenging Angel.

# I Go into the Laboratory

"I go into the laboratory and God tells me what to do," said George Washington Carver, famous Negro scientist. He produced some three hundred by-products from the humble peanut and a hundred or more from the sweet potato. All these he discovered with tools made from junk from a scrap heap.

In a letter, he once wrote words to the effect that he had found that his part in all this manifestation was to *listen* and not tell God what to do. When he entered his laboratory from which such wonders were to proceed, he began to listen. He was following out the command to listen and hear what the Lord has to say unto the temples.

You are a temple of the living God through which many wonders are to come forth, but if you are so busy trying to get things, your mind is so filled with desires that nothing can be heard and nothing can happen but the "inventions" of human thought.

Man has worked out many inventions; he has caused them to happen by his psychological handling of God. He has affirmed and declared and demanded that God give him certain desires of his heart instead of listening in the silence and hearing, "I will give you the desires of your heart." 'The heart that is purified is not trying to get things; it is too busy accepting the manifestations that fall in a never-ceasing stream—more than you ask or think.

The silent approach is filled with awe and wonder, and when the impulsion begins to come through, the manifestations begin to appear. It is wonderful what the sealed lips can say and the silent heart can proclaim. The moment you get beyond the agonizing calling upon the Lord, you will hear Him calling on you and will experience the flow of Life and Power through your temple. That will be enough.

It is all so simple and so void of taking thought, yet it is eschewed by most people, who believe they can declare the unseen into visibility by the use of words or formulae.

"I go into the laboratory and God tells me what to do." I go to pray and receive instructions and revelation, not to convince God. I can wait on the Lord, for He is the only one who can bring it to pass.

Ways and means are in the keeping of the impulsion of God through the temple-man. Go into your laboratory and find out some of the new and wonderful experiences and revelations that he is going to bring out through you. In a split-second, the power has telescoped the time-space of human belief and shown you things which eyes have not seen, nor ears heard, but which are to be projected through your laboratory.

# About the Author

Walter Lanyon was highly respected as a spiritual teacher of Truth. He traveled and lectured to capacity crowds all over the world, basing his lectures, as he said, "solely on the revelation of Jesus Christ."

At one point, he underwent a profound spiritual awakening, in which he felt "plain dumb with the wonder of the revelation." This enlightening experience "was enough to change everything in my life and open the doors of the heaven that Jesus spoke of as here and now. I know what it was. I lost my personality; it fell off of me like an old rag. It just wasn't the same anymore."

His prolific writings continue to be sought out for their timeless message, put forth in a simple, direct manner, and they have much to offer serious spiritual seekers.

Walter Clemow Lanyon was born in the U.S. on October 27, 1887, and he passed away in California on July 4, 1967.

Printed in Great Britain
by Amazon